Lord, I Need Answers

KAY ARTHUR
DAVID ARTHUR

HARVEST HOUSE PUBLISHERS
EUGENE, OREGON

Cover by Koechel Peterson & Associates, Inc., Minneapolis, Minnesota

LORD, I NEED ANSWERS
Rerelease of *Lord, Help Me Grow Spiritually Strong in 28 Days*
Copyright © 2009 by Kay Arthur and David Arthur
Published 2013 by Harvest House Publishers
Eugene, Oregon 97402
www.harvesthousepublishers.com

Library of Congress Cataloging-in-Publication Data
    Arthur, Kay.
    Lord, I Need Answers / Kay Arthur and David Arthur.
        p. cm.
    ISBN 978-0-7369-5156-2 (pbk.)
    ISBN 978-0-7369-5157-9 (eBook)
    1. Spiritual formation. I. Arthur, David, 1967- II. Title.
    BV4511.A78 2009
    248.4—dc22

                                                      2009014591

Printed in the United States of America

13 14 15 16 17 18 19 20 21 / BP-JH / 10 9 8 7 6 5 4 3 2

Praise for
Lord, I Need Answers

There has never been a more critical time for Christians to develop spiritual muscle than now! This dynamic mother–son duo *shows us how* to strengthen our spiritual walk through the "hands-on" process we've come to expect from the master of the inductive method—Kay Arthur. Here's a powerful approach to help people grow spiritually strong...by getting them into the powerful Word of God.

—JUNE HUNT
Founder, CEO, CSO (Chief Servant Officer), Hope for the Heart
Author of *Keeping Your Cool...When Your Anger Is Hot*

David Arthur states that "the Bible isn't just a guidebook...it's an amazing portrait of the Guide Himself." This is a tremendous truth. David, along with his mother, Kay, places precision markers on a variety of passages that the Holy Spirit will open up to those who take Bible study seriously. In a day when Christians seem perplexed about what God's Word really teaches, this book comes alive when measured against God's truth. I agree with Kay that "it's obedience to the Word of God that makes us spiritually strong." Applying these lessons will strengthen every believer's walk with Christ.

—FRANKLIN GRAHAM
President and CEO, Billy Graham Evangelistic Association
Samaritan's Purse

Kay Arthur is one of the most inspiring Bible teachers in America...I am sure that Kay's anointed teaching will bring a blessing to you and your family.

—PAT ROBERTSON
Chairman, The Christian Broadcasting Network
Host of *The 700 Club*

I have been so excited about the Bible studies and books that Kay Arthur has written and...is writing with her son. I highly recommend this book to everyone.

—DEDE ROBERTSON

The Christian life is lived long-term. Day by day—even moment by moment. Kay and David lay out a plan that you can follow in purposeful obedience to God's Spirit and His Word. Engage in a process that you'll establish in a short time but can faithfully and fruitfully live out the rest of your life.

—DR. JAMES MACDONALD
Senior pastor, Harvest Bible Chapel
Bible teacher, *Walk in the Word*

No one I have known in my lifetime has led more of God's people into a richer and more practical understanding of His timeless Word than Kay Arthur. Kay has made the Bible come alive for millions! Now she teams up with her son, David, to show the reader how possible it is to grow spiritually strong in a short amount of time. Every follower of Jesus, whether a newcomer or old-timer, needs the life-changing spiritual challenge of *Lord, I Need Answers*.

—**Dick Eastman**
International president, Every Home for Christ

Lord, I Need Answers is for anyone and everyone who wants to take a step forward from where you are now in terms of understanding the character of God as well as the choices and practices that build up our spiritual muscles for living out the Christian life. David Arthur and his mom, Kay, make a great team in using their personal stories and clear teaching styles to get across essential truths in lessons that won't take all day but will last a lifetime.

—**Nancy Guthrie**
Author of *Hearing Jesus Speak into Your Sorrow*

Kay Arthur and David Arthur take you on a journey that explores an array of biblical themes, real-life issues, and spiritual disciplines that are vital to every child of God. In this interactive resource, they share transparently out of their own pilgrimage, guide you into the Word to discover God's wisdom, and provide the practical help and impetus you need to experience freedom, fullness, and fruitfulness in your walk with Christ.

—**Nancy Leigh DeMoss**
Author, radio host of *Revive Our Hearts*

Kay Arthur writes like she speaks—no frills, no excuses—just plain, direct teaching that changes lives. You'll be helped with this study. Use it and then share it with your friends.

—**Dr. Erwin W. Lutzer**
The Moody Church, Chicago

Contents

Before You Begin 5

1. Is Anyone Really Up There? 7
2. So Who Is God? 13
3. How Can There Be Three in One? 23
4. Who Is the Mysterious Third Person? 31
5. What Purpose Does the Bible Play in My Life? 39
6. How Does the Bible Impact My Life Today? 47
7. Is the Sabbath Rest for Today? If So, How? 55
8. What Happens When I Pray? 63
9. Doesn't My Past Mess Everything Up? Am I Doomed? .. 77
10. Me? Chosen by God? When? 93
11. What Does Grace Have to Do with Me? 99
12. Explain to Me Unconditional Love 105
13. How Am I to Love Others? And Why? 113
14. Is There a Cross in Your Life? 123
15. Holiness? For Me? 129
16. Is Holiness a Process? 139
17. What Is Spiritual Warfare? 145
18. How Is My Mind Like a Battleground? 155
19. Trials: How Am I Supposed to Get Through Them? ... 167
20. I Have Sinned. Again. Now What? 179
21. Is There Any Help for My Sexual Temptations? 191

22. Facing Death—What Should I Do?..................... 201

23. Is There Victory over Fear?........................... 215

24. Am I Supposed to Be Generous?...................... 223

25. Do I Have a Spiritual Gift? 235

26. Does God Still Like the Church? Why?............... 247

27. Don't Walk by Sight? Then How? 253

28. What Is So Great About Being a Slave? 265

Notes... 279

Before You Begin

The bookstores are filled with books that will teach you about growing healthy and getting strong. It seems there are literally thousands of diet and exercise programs that promise to give you "the body you've always wanted." We find it funny that many of these books contradict each other about proper nutrition and weight control. Book One claims one method, and then Book Two comes along and refutes everything Book One so confidently asserted. And then Book Three comes along and says they're both bunk!

This book, however, is about growing strong *spiritually*, not physically. You'll find each day packed with proven methods and timeless principles to enhance your spiritual growth—and they're all founded on the authority of the Word of God, which means they are also true. We have left out our opinions and stuck with the facts.

We must warn you, though, that this isn't a book you simply read. This book requires your participation to make it really worth the time. It is a study—an inductive study. Inductive Bible study is simply a method that enables you to use the Bible as your primary source for information. Throughout this practical book, you will *observe* the text, seeing what it says. You will *interpret* the text, discovering what it means. Finally, you will *apply* the text to your own life.

Even though we haven't met, we want you to know that we have prayed for you. Our prayer is that over the next 28 days, you will experience growth in your spiritual life. We are asking that God will meet you in His Word each day—and strengthen you spiritually. Our desire is that your growth will be like that of a tree planted by streams of water, bursting with fruit!

How blessed is the man who does not walk in the counsel
   of the wicked,
Nor stand in the path of sinners,
Nor sit in the seat of scoffers!
But his delight is in the law of the LORD,
And in His law he meditates day and night.
He will be like a tree firmly planted by streams of water,
Which yields its fruit in its season
And its leaf does not wither;
And in whatever he does, he prospers.

Psalm 1:1-3

Is Anyone Really Up There?

David

I s it really possible to talk to God?

Some people seem to think that's a very strange idea—as though you were slightly unbalanced for even trying. Other people speak casually about long, word-for-word conversations with Him ("and then He said, and then I said...")—as though they had been talking to a friend in the produce aisle of the local grocery store or chatting with a neighbor over the back fence.

I think I've always *wanted* to talk to God—almost as far back as I can remember. But was I doing it right? Saying it correctly? And was He actually listening? Or did He even care about the prayers of a little boy?

Somewhere along the line, I got the idea that I had to start every prayer with a complete confession of every sin I could think of or remember and then beg for forgiveness. I pictured a God who was always just a little angry and more than a little disgusted with me, and I somehow thought He wouldn't pay attention to me at all unless and until I first uttered the words, "God, please forgive all my sins." That, I believed, was the magical phrase that would open the doors of heaven and (finally) get God's attention.

Looking back now on my prayers as a young boy and then as a teenager, they seem more like superstition than a vital part of a relationship with God. Can you relate to such feelings? Does talking to God require a password? If so, what is it? What do I have to say or do to get Him to answer me and help me with my needs? And why does it seem that when I dial His number, He puts me on hold—or doesn't even pick up the phone?

Is He there? Is He listening? Does He actually care about me, my problems, my dreams, my anxieties, and my heartaches?

A DAY OF CHANGE

I can remember worrying about these things—and the sad, empty, almost lonely feeling that came over me as I wondered about God and whether He loved me.

I also remember the day everything changed.

I was at teen Boot Camp, on the campus of Precept Ministries International in Chattanooga, Tennessee. Of course, this was home ground for me. As the son of Jack and Kay Arthur, I'd grown up on that campus and knew every inch of its 32 acres. This particular camp was pretty typical, as far as Precept teen summer camps went. The days were filled with studying the Bible, playing softball and volleyball, singing around the campfire…and Brother Al.

Brother Al, I recall, had been teaching on heaven and hell. It was good stuff, but it wasn't the teaching that bowled me over. And even though I learned some new things in the Bible about what happens after we die, that wasn't what rocked my world. What stunned me that summer was Brother Al's prayers. It was the way he talked to God.

Of course I'd been around innumerable people who prayed out loud through my growing-up years. But for whatever reason, the *reality* of this man's prayers cut through the fog of familiarity and sameness and I've-heard-all-this-before to shake me into alertness. He wasn't just filling the air with churchy sounding words, He was literally *talking to God.*

There could be no doubt. Suddenly, I realized that this man was in live conversation with the Creator of the universe. He had picked up the phone, and *God* was on the line! Of course I'd heard Brother Al pray before. Many times. It wasn't that *he* was doing anything different, it was something happening in *me.* Something supernatural.

It was as if a hood was being lifted from my head—a hood of blindness, suffocation, and deceit.

Now I could see. Really see.

Two things happened to me in very quick order. First, I got it. God is real. Everything I had learned about Him from my parents, school, and church was legitimate. He is alive! Not a superstition or a system of beliefs or a bunch of syrupy, feel-good clichés that no one really believes. God is for real. Immediately after that thought, this next realization hit me—and the impact was like a punch in the stomach.

I really don't know this person Brother Al is talking to. I don't know God.

I'd had enough biblical teaching to know I was in big trouble. If I had walked off campus that night and been hit by a truck out on Noah Reid Road, I was doomed, destined to spend eternity in the lake of fire—in hell with the devil. Images of burning flesh filled my mind, deeply frightening me.

But more than being scared, I now felt guilt. Truckloads of it. Mountains of it. Disgust and nausea took over, and I started to cry. Not a "tear up and bow my head" cry, but an open-mouthed, painful cry. I needed help.

People around me noticed my dilemma. Several thought something was wrong with me and called my parents, who lived on the property. The next several minutes were life-changing. It seemed as though a backpack filled with a heavy load of pretending—faking the Christian life, playing the game—suddenly fell off my back. Just that quickly, the heavy burden was gone. I can't begin to describe to you how free I felt!

A quarter-mile long road loops around the campus at Precept Ministries, and that clear summer night I started to run. But this time I wasn't running from God. I wasn't running from shame or guilt. With a genuine smile on my face, I was running because God had set my heart free!

Later on I found the verse that expressed what I experienced in my conversion: "I run in the path of your commands, for you [God] have set my heart free" (Psalm 119:32 NIV).

FREE AT LAST!

I'm still running. I'm still free!

How about you? Are you free? When you talk to God, does He listen? Does He answer? Or is there so much background noise in your mind that it keeps you from tuning in to what God is saying? Do you feel as though you can't stop moving long enough to really listen for God's voice?

Or maybe your past was so messed up you think that God can't look at you because of evil things you've done or said. If this is your struggle, you won't want to miss what my mother, Kay Arthur, says later in the book about her own story.

I don't know where you are in your life as you read these words, or what you might have experienced as you've thought about God or perhaps tried to talk to Him or get closer to Him. One thing I know—you wouldn't be reading a book with a title like this unless you truly did feel such a desire and hunger in your heart. Something is stirring. Something within you is reaching out for change, for hope, for new strength and understanding.

So let me encourage you with some good news. That stirring you feel in your heart is from God Himself! He is the one who caused this book to be in your hands at this particular season in your life. It's true. And He wants you to draw near to Him more than you ever thought of wanting to draw near to Him. I can tell you, with confidence, that this book and this study will be an important step in that journey.

Not only is God real, alive, and on the throne of heaven and earth, but He desires to be in a tight, authentic, consistent relationship with you. Amazing? You'd better believe it. And if it's really true that God desires to talk and walk with us through everyday life—traffic jams, family fights, addictive temptations, huge disappointments—*then* we have a good opportunity to take hold of life that is truly life (1 Timothy 6:19).

Take some time to reflect on where you are with God. Perhaps start a journal and begin by writing out your own story. Something special occurs when we write out our thoughts and experiences.

In doing research for this book, I asked our Precept leaders to share the most significant lessons they learned in the first 90 days after they became a Christian. To be honest, I was a little surprised by the response I got from that request. The Internet forum was flooded with testimonies. These leaders told of forgiveness, freedom, and excitement about how the Bible began to open up to them and speak to them in deeply personal ways. Many of them described the blessing they received by the simple exercise of writing down their story and sending it to us.

Take Away

In every day of this 28-day study, we will give you a "take away," a practical exercise to help make the main point of each day's lesson stick.

So for today, write out your story. Write down how you came to know Jesus as your Lord and Savior. Be sure to capture how you were drawn to God and what happened when you came to know Him for who He really is. Include the changes that followed in your life. Since God's Word is "living and active and sharper than any two-edged sword" (Hebrews 4:12), be sure to pack your testimony with relevant Scriptures.

Now with your story written, ask God to show you who He wants you to tell your story to. Be ready—the opportunity could come very soon.

So Who Is God?

DAVID

Have you ever mistaken someone's identity? It's so embarrassing when you miss all the clues staring you in the face and then open your mouth and say things you regret!

My brother-in-law Oscar had just finished his PhD, so we had a big party to celebrate his achievement. Oscar and Marty, my sister-in-law, have friends from seemingly every country in the world. The party was like a United Nations convention, and I found myself mingling with Africans, Asians, Latinos, and Europeans.

I was making small talk with a young couple, and when I introduced myself to them, they told me they were the Michelins. I asked the dark-haired young man with a strange accent where he worked.

He answered with a shy grin, "Michelin Tire Company."

"Michelin?" I said. "That is funny! I'll bet you get all kinds of comments at work about having the same last name as the founders!"

My wife recognized the obvious and quickly squeezed my hand. Did I get the hint? No, I went on talking about how funny it would be to "pretend to be one of *the* Michelins at work."

The more I talked, the worse it got. Mr. Michelin was getting uncomfortable with the conversation and eventually exited gracefully. After the couple walked away, my wife looked at me in horror. "David! That *was* a Michelin—*the* Michelin family—who own the tire company!"

Oops! Mistaken identity.

Who Is God?

Relationships don't work well if the people involved don't really know each other. If we are to grow strong in the Lord, we must start with an understanding of who God really is.

Why start with identities? Because many of our problems in understanding the Christian life can be traced back to a basic misunderstanding of who God is. It doesn't have to be that way. God has revealed everything we need to know about Him—His personality, His character, His desires, His longings, and His timeless precepts— between the two covers of the book we call the Bible.

Often described as God's Word, the Bible contains 66 different books written by 40 authors and covers thousands of years of history. Yet every single word is ultimately God's. Nothing can be added to make it better, and certainly nothing can be taken away because it is untrue or useless. All of it—in part, and as a whole—is God's perfect and powerful revelation of Himself.

Most of the Bible contains narrative—true stories about God and His interaction with His men, women, and children down through the ages. But it's not all stories. There's poetry, history, drama, down-to-earth counsel for living, and letters from church leaders to friends and to churches across wide swaths of the world.

Who Does the Bible Say God Is?

With all this in mind, doesn't it make sense that if we are to grow in our relationship with God, we start by getting to know who He is? Who *He* says He is?

Who is God? What is He like?

Read the biblical passages printed out below and simply mark every reference to God. Marking helps you quickly identify key people and key words. We suggest you color the word *God* in yellow or draw a triangle over every mention of Him. Don't miss the pronouns that refer to God. After you have marked the text, go back and make a list of what you learn about Him. Simply ask with each marking, What does this say about God? Then let the text itself provide you with the answer.

The best way to let the text speak for itself is to use words right out of the passage. Doing this simple exercise throughout the Bible can be life changing. In fact, we have found that after teaching people all around the world how to study the Bible, this basic question—What do I learn about God?—is useful anytime you are reading the Bible. You will be amazed at what you learn about your heavenly Father if you ask this question each time you study His Word. We encourage you to do this exercise with your Bible using colored pencils. It will make *God* standout on the pages of your Bible, making it easier to get to know Him through reading His Word.

In this first passage God is speaking to Cyrus, King of Persia, who at the time of Isaiah's prophecy hadn't even been born! Cyrus would (eventually) conquer Babylon and let the Jewish people who were being held in captivity return to Jerusalem to rebuild the temple.

Isaiah 45:5-7

5 "I am the LORD, and there is no other;

   Besides Me there is no God.

   I will gird you, though you have not known Me;

6 That men may know from the rising to the setting of

      the sun

   That there is no one besides Me.

   I am the LORD, and there is no other,

7 The One forming light and creating darkness,

   Causing well-being and creating calamity;

   I am the LORD who does all these."

Psalm 103:19

> The LORD has established His throne in the heavens,
>
> And His sovereignty rules over all.

Jeremiah 32:17-19,27

17 "Ah Lord GOD! Behold, You have made the heavens and the earth by Your great power and by Your outstretched arm! Nothing is too difficult for You,

18 who shows lovingkindness to thousands, but repays the iniquity of fathers into the bosom of their children after them, O great and mighty God. The LORD of hosts is His name;

19 great in counsel and mighty in deed, whose eyes are open to all the ways of the sons of men, giving to everyone according to his ways and according to the fruit of his deeds..."

27 "Behold, I am the LORD, the God of all flesh; Is anything too difficult for Me?"

Deuteronomy 32:3-4

3 "For I proclaim the name of the LORD;
  Ascribe greatness to our God!

4 "The Rock! His work is perfect,
  For all His ways are just;

A God of faithfulness and without injustice,

Righteous and upright is He."

Deuteronomy 32:39

"See now that I, I am He,

And there is no god besides Me;

It is I who put to death and give life.

I have wounded and it is I who heal,

And there is no one who can deliver from My hand."

Revelation 4:11 (I love the scene that this verse comes from. Read the chapter to get a feel for the awe and reverence given to God.)

"Worthy are You, our Lord and our God, to receive

glory and honor and power; for You created all things,

and because of Your will they existed, and were

created."

1 Corinthians 8:4-6

4 Therefore concerning the eating of things sacrificed to idols, we know that there is no such thing as an idol in the world, and that there is no God but one.

5 For even if there are so-called gods whether in heaven or on earth, as indeed there are many gods and many lords,

6 yet for us there is but one God, the Father, from whom

are all things and we exist for Him; and one Lord,
Jesus Christ, by whom are all things, and we exist
through Him.

Romans 11:33-36 (This benediction-like paragraph serves as a
hinge that connects the first 11 chapters of Romans, which are
filled with solid, everlasting statements or doctrines about righteousness, with the last 5 chapters, which apply all those eternal
truths to life today.)

33 Oh, the depth of the riches both of the wisdom and
knowledge of God! How unsearchable are His judg-
ments and unfathomable His ways!

34 For who has known the mind of the Lord, or who
became His counselor?

35 Or who has first given to Him that it might be paid
back to Him again?

36 For from Him and through Him and to Him are all
things. To Him be the glory forever. Amen.

In the space below or in your journal, record what you see the text saying about God.

What I learned about God:

If the whole Bible can be described as God's revealing of Himself to mankind, we have barely scratched the surface, haven't we? But we have to start somewhere. *And wherever we start, that's where God's blessing will begin in our lives.*

Take a minute to look at your notes. Let who God is sink into your mind. God wants us to know who He really is. As Christians we don't have to take classes in comparative religions and evaluate all the gods of this world, comparing and contrasting them to one another. We don't have to experiment with each one to see if what it offers is true or not. Using the Bible, we have direct access to the *one true* and *living* God!

Why waste time—and precious days and years of our lives—looking in any other direction?

No Comparison to the True God

God tells the prophet Isaiah, "'To whom then will you liken Me that I would be his equal?' says the Holy One" (Isaiah 40:25). The answer is clear—there is no other God but God!

Now why is that important? Why is it crucial to believe there is only *one* God in the universe and that this God has described

Himself in the pages of the Bible? The answer is as simple as it is profound.

We are fed lies upon lies that all religions are equally valid or that all roads lead to God. In other words, a person can take the path of meditation via the practices of Hinduism or keep the strict laws of the Koran or follow whatever it is he or she has decided to worship. It's all "spirituality," and it all leads to the same place.

Is that true?

No.

How could it be, when these varied religions contradict one another at almost every turn! The Bible tells us there is *only one true* God and that He has revealed Himself and the path to a relationship with Himself through the Bible. The only way to know God and to reach God is to discover what He says about Himself in the Bible.

A New Name—A New Identity

My wife's older brother is the kindest and gentlest person I have ever met. If you ever have the opportunity to meet him, you'll sense his tender heart and outgoing kindness within mere seconds. Joe has Down Syndrome and the intelligence level of a three-year-old. He is about five feet tall and has blond hair and sweet blue eyes.

The day of our wedding Joe kept saying one phrase over and over again. It was obviously very important to him, but at the time we had no idea what he was talking about. In fact, it took us weeks, maybe even months, before my wife and I finally understood what Joe had meant.

"Margaret's name," he told us, "is David."

If he said it once, he said it a score of times. What was he thinking? What had he wanted to express? We (finally) figured it out, and after we did, *we* felt like the ones who had been "slow." Joe's mother had told him that his sister, Margaret Mcgown, was no longer going to be a Mcgown but was going to be an Arthur—Margaret Arthur.

Joe and I are good buddies. He always calls me either David Arthur Arthur Arthur (three times, for emphasis, I guess), or he simply calls me Arthur. But Joe's wedding day proclamation was profound. Margaret was no longer a Mcgown— she was now an Arthur. "Margaret's name is David." Margaret had been given a new name, a new identity.

The same could be said of you. If you are a believer in God, you are no longer your old self. You now belong to God! The Bible tells us very clearly in 1 Corinthians 6:19-20 that "you are not your own... For you have been bought with a price." We will learn in the next few chapters just how you were bought, but for now let's think about the fact that your identity has changed. Your identity, if you are a believer, is now connected to God's identity—the very same God we've been reading about.

Just as my wife's identity is now deeply connected to mine, you are now a possession of the almighty Creator—the one, true, unfathomable, all-powerful God!

Take Away

Who is God? Review what you learned about Him today by listing the facts you uncovered out of the biblical text. With each characteristic you list about God, think about how His attributes affect you in your daily life. Finally, take some time and thank Him for who He is. Be specific. Be honest.

As you close out your time of study today, why not commit to memory one of the verses we have studied together? I think I will memorize Revelation 4:11. How about you?

How Can There Be Three in One?

David

Instead of us introducing you to each of the three persons of God—the Father, the Son, and the Holy Spirit—it would be better to let the Father Himself introduce the other members of the Trinity to you.

We have learned over the years working with hundreds of thousands of students that marking the key words of the biblical text, writing out answers to questions, and even reading the text out loud significantly increase learning.

Who Is the Only Son of God?

Let's start today by taking a look at Luke 3:21-22. Mark in a unique way the references to *Jesus*, the *Holy Spirit*, and *God the Father*. Be sure not to miss the pronouns for each person of the Trinity. I like to use a red cross for Jesus, a blue cloud for the Holy Spirit, and a yellow triangle for God the Father. Or you could simply color all references to God in yellow.

> 21 Now when all the people were baptized, Jesus was also baptized, and while He was praying, heaven was opened,
>
> 22 and the Holy Spirit descended upon Him in bodily form like a dove, and a voice came out of heaven, "You are My beloved Son, in You I am well-pleased."

How is the relationship described in this text between—

Jesus and the Holy Spirit? What happens between the two of them?

Jesus and God the Father?

Later on in Luke 9, we read about Jesus appearing in a supernatural and glorious state with two others, Moses and Elijah, on a mountaintop. Quickly Peter comes up with an idea:

33 And as these were leaving Him, Peter said to Jesus, "Master, it is good for us to be here; let us make three tabernacles: one for You, and one for Moses, and one for Elijah"—not realizing what he was saying.

34 While he was saying this, a cloud formed and began to overshadow them; and they were afraid as they entered the cloud.

35 Then a voice came out of the cloud, saying, "This is My Son, My Chosen One; listen to Him!"

Knowing what you learned earlier in Luke, what similarities do you see in this passage? How is Jesus described? To whom do you think the voice belongs?

Could Jesus Really Be Who He Claimed to Be?

Peter reflects on this event in his letter later on in 2 Peter 1:16-17:

16 For we did not follow cleverly devised tales when we made known to you the power and coming of our Lord Jesus Christ, but we were eyewitnesses of His majesty.

17 For when He received honor and glory from God the Father, such an utterance as this was made to Him by the Majestic Glory, "This is My beloved Son with whom I am well-pleased."

Here is the point: Jesus is the Son of God; God Himself says so.

Not only is Jesus the Son of God, but He is also one with God. By that I mean Jesus *is* God. In John 10, Jesus describes Himself as a good shepherd who cares for His flock, meaning believers in God. A shepherd was responsible for his sheep's safety. He had to keep them safe from predatory animals or even from other shepherds who might steal them. Jesus says that His Father, God, has given Him sheep, and no one is able to snatch them out of His (Jesus') hand.

How could Jesus say such a thing? Did He realize the import of His words—that He was in essence claiming equality with God Himself?

In John 5:18-23, Jesus engages in a hot debate with the Pharisees, the self-appointed religious overseers of the Jews during Jesus' lifetime. Jesus had just healed a lame man, thrilling and amazing all who had witnessed this mighty miracle. The Pharisees, however, were furious. Why? Because the miracle occurred on the Sabbath, the holy day, and the Pharisees' interpretation of the law kept them from doing almost anything on the Sabbath—even a good thing like healing a lame man.

I always feel sad reading about the Pharisees. Here were intelligent, highly educated men who had supposedly dedicated their whole lives to learning about God, serving Him, and guarding His reputation. And yet here was God Himself, in the person of Jesus, right in front of them! He was so close they could have reached out to touch Him. They could look directly into His eyes. Yet they couldn't seem to recognize (or allow themselves to recognize) His true identity. They couldn't let go of the long-held belief that the rules of the Torah—the Old Testament laws—were the only way God's kingdom was going to come and rescue the people of Israel.

Read the text below to see what happens. Note how the Bible describes the relationship between Jesus and God the Father. It will help to mark every mention of *Jesus* and mark every mention of *God the Father*.

18 For this reason therefore the Jews were seeking all the more to kill Him, because He not only was breaking the Sabbath, but also was calling God His own Father, making Himself equal with God.

19 Therefore Jesus answered and was saying to them, "Truly, truly, I say to you, the Son can do nothing of Himself, unless it is something He sees the Father doing; for whatever the Father does, these things the Son also does in like manner.

20 "For the Father loves the Son, and shows Him all things that He Himself is doing; and the Father will show Him greater works than these, so that you will marvel.

21 "For just as the Father raises the dead and gives them
  life, even so the Son also gives life to whom He wishes.

22 "For not even the Father judges anyone, but He has
  given all judgment to the Son,

23 so that all will honor the Son even as they honor
  the Father. He who does not honor the Son does not
  honor the Father who sent Him."

Now take a look at what you marked. What do you learn about God? And what do you learn about Jesus? Write down your observations.

In verse 23, Jesus clearly—beyond all argument—claims equality with God the Father. But did you notice the flow of responsibility in verse 19? Jesus does what He sees the Father doing. He does nothing of Himself. Jesus then is not "another God," but is one with His Father.

JESUS IS EQUAL TO GOD THE ALMIGHTY

This claim of equality with the God of Israel wasn't received well by the Pharisees. Not at all! Read John 10:30-33 and mark the references to both *Jesus* and *God the Father.*

30 "I and the Father are one."

31 The Jews picked up stones again to stone Him.

32 Jesus answered them, "I showed you many good works

from the Father; for which of them are you stoning Me?"

33 The Jews answered Him, "For a good work we do not stone You, but for blasphemy; and because You, being a man, make Yourself out to be God."

What does Jesus mean in verse 30 by saying that He and His Father are one?

It's so important that you see the point Jesus is making here: Not only is He the Son of God, but He *is* God. They are equal.

So many people are confused with this point. Many believe that Jesus was simply a good moral teacher and that His message was in line with God's. But that would be cutting Jesus short of what He claimed to be, wouldn't it?

WAS HE CRAZY?

I find it interesting to listen to skeptics talk about how Jesus was a great teacher but not divine. My question to them is, If Jesus claimed to be the Son of God and equal to God, and He wasn't, wouldn't He be a fool—a crazy man—and not a great teacher? You can't say that Jesus was just a great moral person and not God. Either His claim to be God was true or He was insane!

If God the Father is God and Jesus the Son is also God, who is the Holy Spirit?

When my girls were young, I would make up bedtime stories to tell them. I would often end the time with an exciting event just about to happen and then stop and ask, "And do you know what happens next?" After a long pause I would say, "I'll tell you tomorrow night." The girls would shriek, "Not again, Daddy! Tell us now! We want to know what happens!"

Well, guess what happens next?

We will talk about who the Holy Spirit is tomorrow.

I suggest that in the meantime you commit to memory the opening of the Gospel of John (John 1:1-3,14), where John refers to Jesus as "the Word."

> 1 In the beginning was the Word, and the Word was
>
> with God, and the Word was God.
>
> 2 He was in the beginning with God.
>
> 3 All things came into being through Him, and apart
>
> from Him nothing came into being that has come
>
> into being.
>
> 14 And the Word became flesh, and dwelt among us, and
>
> we saw His glory, glory as of the only begotten from
>
> the Father, full of grace and truth.

Notice the questions that are answered about Jesus: Who? What? When? and Where? In fact these are the questions you can use when reading any passage of the Bible. In our ministry we call them the "5 Ws and an H"—Who? What? When? Where? Why? and How? Go back to the text above and mark every mention of *Jesus*. Be sure to mark all the synonyms that refer to Him, such as "the Word."

Now go back to each marking and ask the 5 Ws and an H questions. Record below what you learn from asking these questions.

Take Away

What is the single most important question a person can answer?

Jesus asked this question of His disciples in Matthew 16:15, "Who do you say that I am?" There is only one correct answer. Maybe you've heard Jesus spoken of as a kind, gentle teacher. Or maybe as a good man but somewhat confused about His relationship to God.

From what you learned today, who does the Bible say Jesus is? Who do *you* say He is? What do you truly believe about Jesus?

You could consider ten thousand different questions before you turn out the lights and go to bed tonight. But not one of them—not even all of them lumped together—would come close to the importance of this single, most important question.

And the answer?

It will truly change your life.

Who Is the Mysterious Third Person?

DAVID

Growing up I often thought of God the Father as the Big Boss—the gray-haired, distinguished, and rarely smiling man who sits on a white throne. Jesus in my mind's eye was like a big brother—always running interference for me with God the Father. Jesus was a brown-haired, bearded man who had gentle eyes, but with a strength that came from somewhere deep within.

The Holy Spirit (I grew up calling Him the Holy Ghost) was just that—a ghost. You can't see a ghost, you can't touch a ghost, and honestly, I used to think you couldn't relate to a ghost. One author describes the Holy Spirit as a person you can never focus on quite clearly. He was like the sun reflecting off the still waters of a lake: beautiful, but difficult to look at.

The Holy Spirit is the most mysterious member of the Trinity. How does the Bible portray Him?

NOT JUST FOR THEOLOGIANS

Why are we even talking about the Holy Spirit? Shouldn't this kind of talk be reserved for theologians or pastors? Isn't it enough to simply know there *is* a Holy Spirit and leave it at that?

I don't think so.

You will discover that the Holy Spirit's role in your spiritual growth is absolutely primary. By His power and His presence, you will come to know God in a way that will allow you to rest in His presence and walk by His power.

In John 14–16, Jesus tells His disciples that His time on earth is almost up. The time had come for Him to lay down His life and return to His Father in heaven. He tells them—to their dismay—that where He is going they cannot follow (yet).

I don't think you and I can imagine how shocking those words must have been to these men. They had left everything to follow Him. For more than three remarkable years, they had walked with Him, eaten with Him, and shared lodgings with Him. They had witnessed mind-boggling miracles in His presence, heard Him teach as no man had ever taught before, and stood with Him in times of pressure and great peril.

And now He was going to leave? He was departing for some destination where they couldn't follow? What would become of them? Where could they turn? I love the promise He gives them right in the middle of all this talk about leaving—"I will not leave you as orphans."

Orphans. Helpless, frightened children living with great loss.

No, that is not what Jesus had in mind for us. He went on to explain that He would send another person to be with His followers—forever. That person was and is the Holy Spirit. Let's look at the text ourselves. Read each passage below and continue marking the different persons of God as you did yesterday. Although Jesus doesn't use the word *Spirit*, mark the pronouns *He*, *Him*, and the other references to the Spirit.

John 14:15-18

15 "If you love Me, you will keep My commandments.

16 "I will ask the Father, and He will give you another
   Helper, that He may be with you forever;

17 that is the Spirit of truth, whom the world cannot
   receive, because it does not see Him or know Him, but

you know Him because He abides with you and will be in you.

18 "I will not leave you as orphans; I will come to you."

List what you learned about the Holy Spirit from marking this text.

Did you see that the Holy Spirit is called "Helper" in verse 16? What does this suggest His role will be in the lives of Christians?

THE HELPER WHO IS ALWAYS WITH YOU

In John 16:7, Jesus tells the disciples why He must leave and what His plan is for them while He is absent from them: "But I tell you the truth, it is to your advantage that I go away; for if I do not go away, the Helper will not come to you; but if I go, I will send Him to you."

What will the Helper do? Let's look further in this passage and mark every reference to the *Holy Spirit.* Then let's see what we can add to our understanding about the Spirit's role. Write your observations in the list you started above.

John 14:26

> "But the Helper, the Holy Spirit, whom the Father will
> send in My name, He will teach you all things, and
> bring to your remembrance all that I said to you."

John 15:26-27

> 26 "When the Helper comes, whom I will send to you
> from the Father, that is the Spirit of truth who pro-
> ceeds from the Father, He will testify about Me,
>
> 27 and you will testify also, because you have been with
> Me from the beginning."

So far you have seen for yourself that the Holy Spirit is called the Helper. Have you ever thought of Him as *your* Helper? Have you ever called out to Him for help when you didn't know what to do or what to say? Well, He is your Helper, sent by the Father for that specific reason. All you have to do is call out to Him in prayer, and He will come to your aid anytime, anywhere. The Helper, we are told, is the one sent by the Father, in the name of Jesus, to testify (share, teach, demonstrate) about Jesus. And He will help you and me to testify—to share with others—about Jesus.

MORE SPECIFICS

What else does the Holy Spirit do? This is a big question, but for now let's see what we can learn from what John says in chapters 14 through 16.

Below is the text of John 16:7-15. As you read this, I want you to do two things: First, mark every reference to the three persons of God—the *Father*, the *Son*, and the *Holy Spirit*. Be sure to mark them as you did earlier. Second, list out what you see the Holy Spirit doing. Be specific and try to use the words you see in the text. It will help to note the verbs associated with the Holy Spirit. This practice is called *observation* in inductive Bible study. It answers the basic question, What does the text say? By using the words that God uses, you will steer clear of misinterpreting what He says. Add your observations to the list you already started on the Holy Spirit.

7 "But I tell you the truth, it is to your advantage that I go away; for if I do not go away, the Helper will not come to you; but if I go, I will send Him to you.

8 "And He, when He comes, will convict the world concerning sin and righteousness and judgment;

9 concerning sin, because they do not believe in Me;

10 and concerning righteousness, because I go to the Father and you no longer see Me;

11 and concerning judgment, because the ruler of this world has been judged.

12 "I have many more things to say to you, but you cannot bear them now.

13 "But when He, the Spirit of truth, comes, He will guide you into all the truth; for He will not speak on His own initiative, but whatever He hears, He will speak; and He will disclose to you what is to come.

14 "He will glorify Me, for He will take of Mine and will disclose it to you.

15 "All things that the Father has are Mine; therefore I said that He takes of Mine and will disclose it to you."

He Is Not Just for Christians

I want to be sure you don't miss that the Holy Spirit's role is not limited just to us as believers, but that His role extends to the entire world. Did you notice the actions of the Holy Spirit? Coming to dwell within you from the Father, convicting the world concerning sin and righteousness, guiding you in truth, disclosing to you the things of God the Father and God the Son, and ultimately glorifying God. Quite a list!

So many people who claim to be Christians really have no clue who the Holy Spirit is and what His role in their lives looks like. It's a sad fact. Many Christians try to live their lives for their heavenly Father without understanding they have an indwelling almighty Helper.

This is why introductions are important. We don't want you to live one single day without knowing about the beautiful promise of the Holy Spirit and the many wonderful things He will do for you and through you.

Take some time as you close out the day to meditate or even memorize these verses:

John 14:16-17

16 "I will ask the Father, and He will give you another Helper, that He may be with you forever;

17 that is the Spirit of truth, whom the world cannot receive, because it does not see Him or know Him, but you know Him because He abides with you and will be in you."

Take Away

There are times in each one of our lives when we feel lonely or abandoned. On some dark day (or night!) we might tell ourselves, "I'm all alone. There's no one else. No one I can turn to." As a Christian, those words can *never* be true for us. You can know on the authority of God's Word that the Holy Spirit is your resident teacher, dwelling within you. He not only teaches you, but He also guides and comforts you. There is nowhere you can go to escape His presence, and He will never abandon you. Jesus sent the Holy Spirit to you, and He promises that the Spirit will work through you to glorify His Father in heaven.

You may find yourself in any number of strange, surprising, or even frightening situations in the course of your life. But you will never, never find yourself alone.

What Purpose Does the Bible Play in My Life?

David

You and I may meet hundreds or even thousands of people over the course of our lives. Many—perhaps most—leave only a fleeting impression. We may hear their names, shake their hands, and then almost immediately forget who we've just met. And the faces? It's funny (or sad) how they all begin to blur as time goes by.

Then there are those few people you meet and never, never forget.

I can see their faces in my mind's eye at this very moment and know their names immediately: Victor, Jimmy, and Maggie. It's not that these people were physically striking or had such powerful personalities. What I remember about them is what they taught me about the Word of God.

Take Victor, for instance.

God has used this humble, unassuming man to plant thousands of churches across the subcontinent of India. The fact is, vast numbers of people have become Christians through Victor's ministry.

But it wasn't just the numbers that stuck in my memory—all of the new churches, conversions, and baptisms. What I remember most was how he responded to my question about "follow-up materials."

He didn't know what I was talking about.

Excited to meet someone with such a successful evangelistic ministry, I immediately wanted to know how he set about making disciples out of these new believers. How did his leadership team keep these converts "walking the walk" through the days, weeks, and months following their decision to follow Jesus?

So I asked Victor, "What kind of curriculum do you use for discipleship?"

"Curriculum?" Victor looked at my blankly. "What do you mean... curriculum?"

That stopped me for a moment. Didn't all church leaders—particularly successful ones—use follow-up study materials? I said, "You know—what kind of *program* have you set up to teach the new believers about God and their faith?"

"Oh," Victor said. "We simply start in the book of Matthew—just reading and doing whatever it says."

Read and obey. Start on page one, read a chapter—or two, or three—and just set out to do whatever God asks you to do. That certainly simplifies things! And it was evidently working for thousands of earnest Indian believers.

That's why I've remembered Victor. And it's also why I've never forgotten Jimmy. A pastor leading an amazing group of Christians in Texas, Jimmy told me that when he became a believer in Jesus, he figured he should read and obey what Jesus said. His understanding of what he was supposed to do seemed so basic, so elementary, so—dare I say it?—childish.

"I just started reading in Matthew chapter 1. If Jesus said do something, well then, I did it. I obeyed His instructions." Jimmy said that by the end of chapter 6, he was financially broke. Jimmy is not one who I would describe as either childish or broke. To me he seems wise and wealthy—wealthy in the ways of Jesus.

The final stand-out person in recent memory (for the same reason as Victor and Jimmy) is an African lady named Maggie. The incredibly poor children to whom she has devoted her life call her "Momma Maggie." Maggie works in a Muslim country and knows that children will be forced to memorize the Koran once they go to school. So she prepares them in advance by having them memorize

Scripture. This pattern isn't just for the children but for her staff of 1600 as well! During our visit, Maggie and the staff who were there demonstrated their training. They had just finished memorizing Matthew 5, and we sat and listened as together they quoted the entire chapter. Everyone in Maggie's circle of influence reads or listens to the Bible every single day.

What do Victor, Jimmy, and Maggie have in common—other than the fact that their faces and their stories remain in high definition in my memory?

They read and obey the Bible *regularly.*

Bottom line, this *is* discipleship. This is without fail a necessity for the person who desires to grow spiritually strong. And I learned from these three devoted followers of Jesus that you don't need a lot of up-to-date curriculum—or computer programs or charts and graphs or sophisticated techniques—to start people on the road to growth and strength in the Christian life.

But you do need the Bible. And the more, the better.

JUST GIVE ME JESUS…WHICH ONE DO YOU WANT?

Maybe in the back of your mind you find yourself thinking: *Can't I just believe that God is real? Can't I just love Jesus? Why do I need the Bible?* If you find yourself thinking such thoughts, I'd counsel you to remember that as believers—from the time we receive Jesus as Savior and Lord—we are at war. In fact, every one of us enters this world as an enemy of God. We are told in Colossians 1:13 that God has rescued us from the domain of darkness and transferred us into the kingdom of His beloved Son.

Rescued from darkness. Transferred to the kingdom of light.

"In the dark" is a good description of what we are without God. But light changes darkness. Light expels darkness. Light shows us where to go and what to avoid.

Later on in Colossians we are given a warning: "See to it that no one takes you captive through philosophy and empty deception, according to the tradition of men, according to the elementary principles of the world, rather than according to Christ" (Colossians 2:8).

It's quite simple. The world teaches the opposite of what God would have us know and do. Therefore, without the teaching from God, we'll be captives of worldly philosophy and empty deception.

The Apostle Paul Had a Succession Plan

Paul had marching orders—a mission from Jesus Himself—that filled his heart with fire and desire. He preached to the Jews, his own countrymen, whenever he could, but he knew that the Lord had primarily called him to bring the message of salvation to the non-Jewish peoples of the nations. And as far as Paul was concerned, the further out on the frontier, the better. As he told the Roman believers, "I aspired to preach the gospel, not where Christ was already named, so that I would not build on another man's foundation; but as it is written, 'they who had no news of Him shall see, and they who have not heard shall understand'" (Romans 15:20-21).

But Jesus had called Paul not only to preach, He had also called him to suffer for the sake of the gospel. As a result, Paul found himself frequently imprisoned. That was a good outcome for you and me because he wrote much of the New Testament while in Roman chains. But it must have been frustrating for Paul, who so much wanted the gospel to reach farther and farther into the world.

That's why he needed helpers.

Knowing he had to pass on to others the mission Jesus had given to him, Paul picked a young man named Timothy to train for this purpose. This was no overnight, crash-course succession plan. For Timothy, this plan involved literally walking with Paul from town to town sharing the gospel message. After much time one-on-one, Paul then sent his protégé to towns by himself. Often Paul would send letters of instruction and encouragement to the people receiving young Timothy.

But the last letter Paul wrote was written directly to Timothy.

Reading that letter (2 Timothy in our Bibles) gives you two

distinct impressions: One, that Paul knew his end was near and that these might be his last written words, and two, that he loved this young man as a son. And in the four brief chapters, the apostle pours out his heart.

Paul was about to be executed because of his devotion to the mission of Jesus, and he was passing the baton to Timothy. Second Timothy 1:14 captures well the essence of the letter: "Guard, through the Holy Spirit who dwells in us, the treasure which has been entrusted to you." The treasure mentioned was not some pot of gold buried away for retirement; rather, it was the Word of God that Paul had been teaching.

GUARD THE TREASURE

Guard the Word of God, the Bible? How? By hiding it away in a safety deposit box in Switzerland? By burying it away where no one can steal it or alter its message?

No. Actually Paul teaches Timothy that the way to guard the message is by teaching it to others, by living in accordance with what it says, and by handling it accurately. In 2 Timothy 3:16-17, Paul shares the reason why the Bible is so important and why it must be guarded. Read through these two verses and list out everything Paul says about Scripture.

16 All Scripture is inspired by God and profitable for teaching, for reproof, for correction, for training in righteousness;

17 so that the man of God may be adequate, equipped for every good work.

What I learn about Scripture:

GOD-BREATHED SCRIPTURE

Just what is Paul teaching when he says "Scripture is inspired"? The Greek word translated "inspired" means literally "God-breathed." What does God-breathed mean? In all honesty, it's one of the most important questions we could ever consider. It doesn't mean that God dictated the words to Paul for him to simply write them down. ("Take a memo, Paul.") Nor does it mean that God gave Paul an idea, and then Paul expounded on the idea with his own thoughts. Rather "God-breathed"—inspired—means that what the different writers of Scripture recorded on the page, God placed there through the Holy Spirit. The words of the Bible are ultimately the word of God.

Now with your list in mind, answer these questions:

What parts of Scripture are inspired?

How do you know that Scripture is of value?

What is it profitable for? List out each activity.

What can we assume about ourselves knowing that the Bible is useful for reproof and correction? ("Reproof" means to undo incorrect thinking and behavior and realign with the truth.)

Finally, why does Paul say we need the Scriptures? (Hint: read verse 17—the words "so that" usually answer the *why* question.)

If Paul used his final message to prepare Timothy, his apprentice, to guard the treasure, the Word of God, then what are the applications to you and me as followers of God? How should we think of the Bible? What is it useful for in our lives?

So Show Me Where to Begin

I can imagine that some of you are now a bit worried. You may be worried because you really don't know *how* to study your Bible. It may be foreign to you, and you may not know how to get started. Well, lay your fears aside. Kay has written a book called *Lord, Teach Me to Study the Bible in 28 Days,* and I recommend you read it after you finish this one.

If it is not your habit to take time daily to read, study, and meditate on Scripture, we encourage you to start today. Psalm 1:1-3 tells us that the person who delights in the law of the Lord and meditates on it daily is "blessed" and is like a tree firmly planted by streams of water. A great passage of Scripture to study and even memorize is Hebrews 4:12:

> For the word of God is living and active and sharper than any two-edged sword, and piercing as far as the division of soul and spirit, of both joints and marrow, and able to judge the thoughts and intentions of the heart.

Think of how powerful the Word of God is! Think about what it can do in your life.

Take Away

We all enter this world as damaged goods, unable to discern truth from error on our own. We need help, and we need it daily. We simply can't trust our own "gut" to guide us. No matter how logical or "right" that way might feel to us, in the end we won't like the destination. Solomon wrote: "There is a way which seems right to a man, but its end is the way of death" (Proverbs 14:12). Our God, however, has provided just the help we need in His Word, the Bible. It is the ultimate GPS system, teaching us the right paths to choose in life and showing us the way to life everlasting beyond the grave! Make a commitment to read it regularly. We suggest you set aside time each day. Start today and you will begin to see how life-changing fellowship with God is through His Word. You truly will be blessed, as the psalmist declares.

How Does the Bible Impact My Life Today?

David

I was so excited I could hardly sleep! I lay in my bed with my eyes wide open and reviewed my packing list: Paddle (my favorite, handmade from ash wood)—*check*. My trusty helmet (with battle wounds from striking underwater rocks)—*check*. My life vest, kayak skirt, and river-running kayak, "The White Dancer"—*check*.

Okay, now it's time to sleep. But I couldn't.

A Guide Book That Is Alive

That week I had read a guidebook about the Chattooga River, written by an experienced kayaker who had paddled the river many times. The book not only described the specific paths a paddler must take in each rapid, but also told the "crash-and-burn" stories of people getting pinned between rocks, of broken shoulders, and yes, of death. The author's intention was to show readers how to really enjoy the river for themselves—and live through the experience. The book was filled with specifics, ranging from where to park your car to how to avoid disaster in certain rapids. It was not only an instructional book but also a book of encouragement.

So why was I having trouble sleeping?

Somehow, just having all the information about running the river wasn't enough. I needed something more. Then I remembered. *I wasn't running the river alone.* I was running it with Chris.

Chris is an amazing kayaker. I had paddled with him many times before in various rivers. He had a gift. Chris would do things with his boat that seemed to have more to do with flying than with river running. He had a sense of the river—where to go and not go, how to approach a rapid, what to do when in trouble, and how to maximize the joy and thrill factor in every circumstance. Treacherous rapids weren't obstacles to Chris, they were opportunities.

I'm going with Chris on the Chattooga...that was my last thought as I finally drifted asleep.

Read Luke 8:22-25:

> 22 Now on one of those days Jesus and His disciples got into a boat, and He said to them, "Let us go over to the other side of the lake." So they launched out.

> 23 But as they were sailing along He fell asleep; and a fierce gale of wind descended on the lake, and they began to be swamped and to be in danger.

> 24 They came to Jesus and woke Him up, saying, "Master, Master, we are perishing!" And He got up and rebuked the wind and the surging waves, and they stopped, and it became calm.

> 25 And He said to them, "Where is your faith?" They were fearful and amazed, saying to one another, "Who then is this, that He commands even the winds and the water, and they obey Him?"

Why were the disciples afraid? Who *wouldn't* be? Even though most of these men where seasoned, veteran fishermen and had lived around the Sea of Galilee their whole lives, this was one circumstance in which they had never wanted to find themselves. Caught in one of Galilee's fierce, sudden storms, they were in the middle of the sea and water was swamping their boat.

Wasn't it obvious they were only minutes from death?

Or...had they forgotten one very important fact?

Jesus Himself was in the storm with them! The boat wasn't going to sink with the Son of God on board. And through that harrowing experience, they would be reminded of two all-important facts: One, their Master was all-powerful—more than a match for any situation. And two, He was with them through it all. It was His presence that made all the difference.

Sometimes when we think about the Bible and its role in our lives, we think of it as a river guide—a book that warns us of dangers and points out paths of security and safety. And that would be a good comparison: The Bible certainly does contain instructions and warnings we need to know and follow. But it's much more than that.

The Bible is made up of history, poetry, letters, prophecies—66 different books written over a period of perhaps 1600 years with multiple authors, multiple contexts, multiple purposes. And yet they together make one book—the revelation of God. So in that sense the Bible isn't just a guidebook with practical tips on how to survive and enjoy the river we call life; it's an amazing portrait of the Guide Himself.

A Great Rescue Story

Let's look at a story early on in the Bible. The people of God had just been delivered from the most powerful nation on earth—Egypt. Egypt had enslaved the Hebrews and ruled over them with iron fist. For 400 years it seemed as if God had forgotten His own children. Then in Exodus 2:22-25, we read what happens:

> 22 Then she gave birth to a son, and he [Moses] named him Gershom, for he said, "I have been a sojourner in a foreign land."
>
> 23 Now it came about in the course of those many days that the king of Egypt died. And the sons of Israel sighed because of the bondage, and they cried out; and their cry for help because of their bondage rose up to God.
>
> 24 So God heard their groaning; and God remembered His covenant with Abraham, Isaac, and Jacob.

> 25 God saw the sons of Israel, and God took notice of
>   them.

God heard their pain, saw His people in their bondage, and remembered His covenant—His promise to Abraham, Isaac, and Jacob.

The text says, "God took notice of them."

That's a truth that could keep you in a state of awe for the rest of your life. Why should God—Creator of a universe beyond all reckoning or calculation, all-knowing, all-powerful, and eternal—why would such a One as He *take notice* of someone like you or me? We're just the tiniest little flecks of dust on a world that is hardly more than a grain of sand in a seemingly endless cosmos.

Yet He takes notice of each one of us, just as He took notice of His captive people in Egypt.

What follows is an incredible story of rescue. God changed the heart of Pharaoh and caused him to release the Hebrews, sending them off with the amassed gold and treasures of the Egyptian people. He worked supernaturally in the hearts of the Egyptians to give gifts to the departing Hebrew slaves.

I love that story. That is a big God! Not only did He cause the release of His enslaved people, but He sent them off with a going-away present from the enemy—the wealth of the most advanced, powerful nation on earth at that time.

Now that the Hebrew people were released, God sent them on a journey. The journey was to the Promised Land—the territory specified in the covenantal promise God had made centuries earlier to Abraham (Genesis 12:1-3) and repeated many times after that.

But there was a problem—a *huge* problem. How were they to feed themselves? The Bible tells us that 600,000 fighting men emerged from Egypt during that great exodus. So when you add in the women and the children, you would have been talking about two and a half to three million people. In other words, it was like the population of a large city. And where they were going there were no farms, grocery stores, delis, or Golden Arches.

But those sorts of logistics were no trouble for God. He *always* has a plan. He already had in mind how He would feed this nation of people—daily—by delivering bread from heaven, six days a week. It was called "manna," a Hebrew word that means "What is this?" Every day—without fail—God fed them this sweet, nutritious food, and all they had to do was pick it up off the desert floor. He made it very clear to them that they were not to store it, as if it were not going to appear the next day. (God did tell the people not to collect manna on the Sabbath, but instead to collect enough on day six for the seventh day. We'll look at this tomorrow.)

Interestingly, those who refused to trust God and decided to save some manna for the following day discovered that their manna pots were infested with maggots. God was clear—He wanted to feed His people daily.

Read Deuteronomy 8:1-3 and see how God connects His feeding the people with daily bread to listening to and obeying His Word:

> 1 "All the commandments that I am commanding you today you shall be careful to do, that you may live and multiply, and go in and possess the land which the Lord swore to give to your forefathers.

> 2 "You shall remember all the way which the LORD your God has led you in the wilderness these forty years, that He might humble you, testing you, to know what was in your heart, whether you would keep His commandments or not.

> 3 "He humbled you and let you be hungry, and fed you with manna which you did not know, nor did your fathers know, that He might make you understand that man does not live by bread alone, but man lives by everything that proceeds out of the mouth of the Lord."

OUR LIVES DEPEND ON IT

Did you catch what He says at the end of verse 3? Our life depends on God's Word—every single word! Everything that proceeds out of the mouth of the Lord is what sustains us in life.

God didn't simply give us a guidebook filled with instructions.

God didn't merely compile a list of dos and don'ts for living a holy life.

God gave us powerful, true stories, such as the account of the manna in the wilderness. Stories like these demonstrate that we are to hang on every single word that proceeds from His mouth. If we don't, we die.

But God also gave Himself as our guide. Jesus, asleep in the boat, was the disciples' guide. He was with them, and that changed everything. God was with the Hebrews in the wilderness, guiding them and feeding them daily, and that changed everything for them too.

On the river that day I really enjoyed myself. I successfully paddled level 4 and 5 rapids such as "Corkscrew," "Sock-em Dog," and "Shoulder Bone." The secret? Well, for starters, I was an experienced paddler who understood the basics. Second, I had studied the Chattooga guidebook carefully.

But most importantly, I followed Chris.

Chris was my guide—every single second—on that river. I went where he went. I did what he told me to do.

Friend, this is like the relationship we can have with God through His Word, the Bible. It's not some dry reference book that belongs on a dusty shelf. God's Word is alive and powerful, and sticks with us every second of every day. His Word is our life. When we read God's Word, we are listening to God speak to us in the very moment we read. Having God's Word in our hearts and minds is like having Jesus in the boat with us. Having God's Word is like having God rain down exactly what we need every moment of every day.

The Bible isn't just a guidebook. No, it points us to the Guide Himself.

Finish out your time of study this day by meditating on the passage below, and ask God to speak to you—to your life—now.

1 Thessalonians 2:13

> For this reason we also constantly thank God that when you received the word of God which you heard from us, you accepted it not as the word of men, but for what it really is, the word of God, which also performs its work in you who believe.

TAKE AWAY

Are you convinced that the Word is essential for growing spiritually strong? If so, you may still be wondering "Where do I begin?" Here are some ideas for you to consider.

First, finish this book. You have a chapter for every day remaining in our 28-day journey together. Next, a lot of helpful Bible study resources are available from www.Precept.org. Spend some time browsing through those materials.

In the previous chapter I mentioned Kay's helpful book, *Lord, Teach Me to Study the Bible in 28 Days.* You might also want to take a look at *The New Inductive Study Bible,* which provides you with tools for *observing* what the Bible says, *interpreting* what it means, and *applying* it to your life. And Precept Ministries has produced numerous Bible studies, ranging from short topical studies to in-depth studies of entire books of the Bible.

Is the Sabbath Rest for Today?
If So, How?

DAVID

God our Creator started with nothing and finished with everything. In just six days, He created all that exists. But the Genesis story doesn't end with those six days. Another day is recorded in chapter 2. As you read the text below, mark that *seventh day* with the number 7 and see what you learn.

Genesis 2:1-3

> 1 Thus the heavens and the earth were completed, and all their hosts.

> 2 By the seventh day God completed His work which He had done, and He rested on the seventh day from all His work which He had done.

> 3 Then God blessed the seventh day and sanctified it, because in it He rested from all His work which God had created and made.

What did you see about the seventh day? List below what you observed.

Did you notice that this seventh day was to be sanctified? The term "sanctified" literally means it was "set apart" from the other days. The seventh day was to be special. It would later be known as the Sabbath day. "Sabbath" comes from the Hebrew word that means "to stop, cease, rest." So how did God set this day apart from the others? He rested. He ceased His work of creating.

This idea of resting on the seventh day was so important in the flow of life for mankind that God commanded His people to rest, to keep the day set apart, to keep it holy.

REASONS FOR REST

In Exodus 20:8-11, we're given reasons for this command to keep a day of rest. It's interesting to note that this command has the largest description of all of the Ten Commandments connected to it. God says more about this command than any of the others. Does that make it the most important of the commands? No, Jesus made it clear which two commands were most important (see Matthew 22:37-40). But it does give us some indication of its value to God.

8 "Remember the sabbath day, to keep it holy.

9 "Six days you shall labor and do all your work,

10 but the seventh day is a sabbath of the LORD your God; in it you shall not do any work, you or your son or your daughter, your male or your female servant or your cattle or your sojourner who stays with you.

11 "For in six days the LORD made the heavens and the earth, the sea and all that is in them, and rested on the seventh day; therefore the LORD blessed the sabbath day and made it holy."

Let's study this text together. Remember the process we've been using so far. First, we mark the word *Sabbath* and all its pronouns and synonyms. After marking the word, we list what we learn about it.

What we learn about the Sabbath:

REST AND MIRACLES

Did you notice the link between the historical event of creation and the command to keep the Sabbath day holy? Let's back up in the book of Exodus to an earlier mention of *Sabbath* and see what we can learn.

Israel has just taken their exit from Egypt after 400 years of slavery. Led by Moses and Aaron, the people are on their way through an amazingly desolate wilderness en route to the Promised Land.

You would think that the people of Israel would be caught up in over-the-top rejoicing. God—their very own God—had just smashed the gods of Egypt, delivered them from multigenerational servitude, loaded them up with great wealth and treasures untold, and set them on a road trip to the land "flowing with milk and honey."

But they weren't rejoicing at all.

In fact, they were bitterly complaining against the Lord and against Moses.

We discover why God is about do what He does in Exodus 16:4: "Then the LORD said to Moses, 'Behold, I will rain bread from heaven for you; and the people shall go out and gather a day's portion every day, that I may test them, whether or not they will walk in My instruction.'"

God is about to do a miracle—He is going to daily deliver sweet, delicious bread to feed His people. But His provision comes with His commands. This will be a test of whether they will obey God or disobey Him. His instruction to them up to this point had basically been: Gather what you need for that day, no more and no less.

Now, let's read on to see what happens. As you read the text below, mark every mention of *Sabbath*. Also mark the phrase *seventh day* the same way you marked *Sabbath*. After you have read and marked the text below, we will ask some questions.

Exodus 16:22-30

22 Now on the sixth day they gathered twice as much bread, two omers for each one. When all the leaders of the congregation came and told Moses,

23 then he said to them, "This is what the LORD meant: Tomorrow is a sabbath observance, a holy sabbath to the LORD. Bake what you will bake and boil what you will boil, and all that is left over put aside to be kept until morning."

24 So they put it aside until morning, as Moses had ordered, and it did not become foul nor was there any worm in it.

25 Moses said, "Eat it today, for today is a sabbath to the LORD; today you will not find it in the field.

26 "Six days you shall gather it, but on the seventh day, the sabbath, there will be none."

27 It came about on the seventh day that some of the people went out to gather, but they found none.

28 Then the LORD said to Moses, "How long do you refuse to keep My commandments and My instructions?

29 "See, the LORD has given you the sabbath; therefore

He gives you bread for two days on the sixth day.

Remain every man in his place; let no man go out of

his place on the seventh day."

30 So the people rested on the seventh day.

Why were the people to gather twice as much on the sixth day?

How was the seventh day described? Use words from the text as much as possible.

In verse 24 we are told that the extra bread did not spoil. Earlier in this chapter, in verse 20, we see that any extra bread collected on days one through six would spoil overnight. So why do you think the extra bread on night six stayed fresh?

How did God respond to the people who went to gather bread on the Sabbath (verses 27-28)?

The final words of this passage tell us that people rested on the seventh day. Stopped. Ceased from their labors. Set the day apart from the others.

REST IN THE NEW TESTAMENT

The Sabbath day was designed by God to be a day for rest. But for whose benefit? Read Mark 2:23-28 below and list what you learn about the purpose of the Sabbath.

> 23 And it happened that He was passing through the grainfields on the Sabbath, and His disciples began to make their way along while picking the heads of grain.
>
> 24 The Pharisees were saying to Him, "Look, why are they doing what is not lawful on the Sabbath?"
>
> 25 And He said to them, "Have you never read what David did when he was in need and he and his companions became hungry;
>
> 26 how he entered the house of God in the time of Abiathar the high priest, and ate the consecrated bread, which is not lawful for anyone to eat except the priests, and he also gave it to those who were with him?"
>
> 27 Jesus said to them, "The Sabbath was made for man, and not man for the Sabbath.
>
> 28 "So the Son of Man is Lord even of the Sabbath."

What (or whom) is the Sabbath for?

Why Do We Struggle with Rest?

I wish I had learned this lesson earlier on in my years. To stop once a week and commit to a day of rest creates a balance and healthy rhythm to life. God has designed life with a pattern in mind. He wants us to work—to work hard—for His glory six days a week. But He wants to give us something on the seventh day. He wants to give us rest. One of our Jewish friends in Jerusalem, Danny Eliav, says it's the best gift God ever gave to His people.

It takes faith to receive that gift. It takes a firm belief in God as our ultimate provider to take a day off from work. Now I know some of you may think I've gone off the deep end here. Stop work?

Eugene Peterson, a pastor to pastors, wrote about pastors taking a Sabbath in his book *Working the Angles: The Shape of Pastoral Integrity*. I read these words in my first year as a pastor, and the message hit me between the eyes. Peterson wrote: "If you don't take off one day a week—you take yourself far too seriously." Resting is a demonstration of our dependence on God as our provider. Does this concept of resting speak to your fear of provision, your inability to trust God to meet your needs? Or maybe this reveals your assumption that, somehow, "It's all up to you." You know what I mean—that the more *you* work, the more you accomplish for God, for your family, for the bottom line, or whatever.

Our emphasis tends to be on "what we do for God." The emphasis of the New Testament, however, is on what God, through Christ, can accomplish in and through us. Paul reminded us that "it is God who is at work in you, both to will and to work for His good pleasure" (Philippians 2:13).

And six days are more than enough for Him to do everything that needs doing.

Take Away

The lesson for the day is rest. Can you see from what you studied today that God has built a seven-day rhythm into life? He has designed us to both work and rest. This is important for spiritual growth. I don't know how to shout in a book, but if I could, I would shout this now: *Don't try to grow on your own strength! Don't be fooled into thinking that the more you work on growth the more it will happen! Please, please rest!*

Here is what we promise you, friend:

- In rest you will find that you grow in trusting God.
- In rest you will find that you grow in following God and not your own agenda.
- In rest you will find that you grow in strength, and this, my friend, pleases your heavenly Father.

Here are words from the wisest man in history, King Solomon. We suggest you think, chew, wrestle with, and even memorize these words of rest.

Psalm 127:1-2

> 1 Unless the LORD builds the house,
>   They labor in vain who build it;
>   Unless the LORD guards the city,
>   The watchman keeps awake in vain.
>
> 2 It is vain for you to rise up early,
>   To retire late,
>   To eat the bread of painful labors;
>   For He gives to His beloved even in his sleep.

What Happens When I Pray?

David

BALLOONS AND TRAINS

Sometimes mental pictures help us take an abstract thought and make it more concrete. Jesus constantly used such pictures to drive home spiritual truths

Let's try this one on for size: Do you see your life more like a train or a hot-air balloon?

A train? Well, it's a series of connected cars, constructed of hard steel, moving in a linear direction, and inescapably bound to a rigid track. And maybe, in a similar fashion, you find yourself headed in a certain direction, not necessarily by choice but perhaps by circumstances life has dealt you. Perhaps you see yourself as an individual who has been so bent, hardened, and shaped by life that you have simply lost the freedom to choose the path ahead. Have you lost your ability to be flexible? To adapt to changing environments? Have your patterns of living become hardened into habits that are nearly impossible to change?

Or maybe you're more like one of those huge, marvelous hot-air balloons we occasionally see drifting majestically across the sky: soft in form, flexible in shape, easily changed in direction, and letting the wind take you where it may. You have no control of your path each day; you are simply taken where the wind currents decide you should go. You're light, you're free, and you owe no obligation to the rigid tracks far below you.

Honestly, I feel like both. Some days I feel I have an agenda to accomplish, and nothing but nothing is going to get in my way! I *will* get there. Or will I? Doubt creeps into my soul. Yes, I've got a good head of steam going...but am I truly headed in the right direction?

I feel like a train when my habits become my pattern for life. I get on an anger track...or a pride track...or a lust or envy or selfish track.

But what I want to be is a balloon. I want to go wherever the Spirit will take me. I want to respond to His current, His nudges, His moving. I want to live an adventure each day—of not necessarily knowing where I will go, where I will end up. I want to be flexible rather than rigid. I want God to shape me, and to fully cooperate with that shaping process.

BEING MORE BALLOONLIKE

To grow strong as believers, we need to be guided, moved, and shaped by the wind of the Holy Spirit.

But how?

Through prayer. Prayer is one of the best tools God created to shape us, guide us, and move us.

Let's go back to the train image. Iron. Rigid. Stuck on rails. Is that what prayer feels like to you? Stuck in a rut? Chugging along the same old familiar route every day? My prayer time with my girls easily slips into something like this: "Lord, please be with my daughters as they go to school. Please help them to learn more about You, and please keep them safe." Safety is my main concern. But is that all there is? Don't I want something more for their lives than *safety*?

How do we escape the track of rigid, rote, repetitive prayers—prayers that begin to feel like a boring routine rather than speaking to our magnificent God and Father?

Jesus has the answer. In Matthew 6, He teaches His disciples *how* to pray. Verse 1 sets the context for the reader: "Beware of practicing your righteousness before men to be noticed by them; otherwise you have no reward with your Father who is in heaven."

Prayer has nothing to do with impressing other people.

Prayer has nothing to do with impressing God.

It's not as though we need to manipulate God or somehow persuade Him to do our bidding. On the contrary, as we pray to our Father with a humble and submitted heart, *we* are the ones who will be moved, persuaded, taught, comforted, and changed. I'm not the engineer on a train, asking God to "get on board." No, I'm one of those magnificent balloons, being carried along on a heavenly current of air. As I pray, I'm following His thoughts, His desires, His plans and purposes, even as I experience the surrounding freshness of His love.

HOW AM I SUPPOSED TO PRAY?

Read the text below and mark every mention of *prayer* (include all forms of the word and synonyms). In case you are stuck on color or symbol, *The New Inductive Study Bible* (NISB) in its suggested markings has this for prayer: ∽.

Matthew 6:5-8

> 5 "When you pray, you are not to be like the hypocrites;
>
> for they love to stand and pray in the synagogues and
>
> on the street corners so that they may be seen by men.
>
> Truly I say to you, they have their reward in full.
>
> 6 "But you, when you pray, go into your inner room,
>
> close your door and pray to your Father who is in
>
> secret, and your Father who sees what is done in secret
>
> will reward you.
>
> 7 "And when you are praying, do not use meaningless
>
> repetition as the Gentiles do, for they suppose that
>
> they will be heard for their many words.

8 "So do not be like them; for your Father knows what

you need before you ask Him."

Take a moment to note every place where you marked *prayer*, and list what you learned. Be sure to stick with what the text is saying and try not to "read into" the passage things that aren't clearly taught in these verses. We call this "letting the text speak for itself."

Prayer:

So, if we are to avoid using prayer as a platform to perform before God and others, and if we're taught to avoid using meaningless repetition, then what are prayers to be like? What are we to pray? Let's keep reading and marking any references to *prayer*.

Matthew 6:7-13

7 "And when you are praying, do not use meaningless

repetition as the Gentiles do, for they suppose that

they will be heard for their many words.

8 "So do not be like them; for your Father knows what

you need before you ask Him.

9 "Pray, then, in this way: 'Our Father who is in heaven,

Hallowed be Your name.

10 'Your kingdom come. Your will be done, on earth as it

is in heaven.

11 'Give us this day our daily bread.

12 'And forgive us our debts, as we also have forgiven our

  debtors.

13 'And do not lead us into temptation, but deliver us

  from evil. [For Yours is the kingdom and the power

  and the glory forever. Amen.]' "

ORGANIZED OR FREESTYLE?

Most of us have heard of the Lord's Prayer, in verses 7-13. Down through the centuries, people have used these words in different ways—sometimes simply reciting the prayer phrase by phrase, and at other times using the Lord's words as a template, letting them shape and organize and prioritize their conversations with God.

It works either way. We can simply pray this prayer as it is, making each request our own, or we can use it as a guide, keeping our personal prayers on a productive path. Before we explore this second option, though, let's list what we learn about prayer, as we did earlier.

Prayer:

What a list! Isn't it incredible how much we can learn if we simply let the text speak for itself? As I write these words, I'm in the middle of an exercise program. And rather than depending on expensive and complicated machinery, I'm learning how to use my own weight and body to exercise and strengthen my muscles. Inductive Bible study is like that—you don't need piles of dictionaries and commentaries and hours of sermons on a text to grasp its basic message. You simply need to let it speak for itself. Yes, there is certainly a place for all of those study tools I just mentioned. But they should always be *secondary* to using the Bible as your primary source of study.

As you made your list of what you learned about prayer, did you see any "categories" about praying? Guidelines? Structure? If so, write them out below:

How NOT to Start Prayers

Let's start by looking at the general outline of this text. Did you notice how the prayer starts? Or perhaps how it *doesn't* start? Jesus didn't say, "Begin by telling your Father everything you need and want Him to do for you."

No, in verses 9-10, we see that Jesus begins this model prayer with *worship*. And that's where we need to begin as well. Worship is declaring God's worth. Think of it as "worth-ship," and it will be easy to remember. Merriam-Webster's dictionary tells us that the Old English word for worship was *weorthscipe*, meaning "worthiness, respect." Can you see the word "worth" in that Old English word?

Prayer then is to begin with worship—not our grocery list of personal requests. Verse 9 defines who God is—our Father who is in heaven—and then ascribes worth to His name by stating, "Hallowed be Your name." In her book *Lord, Teach Me to Pray in 28 Days*, my mother, Kay, cleverly says that we are not to hollow His name but to *hallow* it. To hollow is to empty the name of its deserved honor and glory—the polar opposite of worship.

Verse 10 tells us that we are to recognize God's kingdom and to pray for its dominion from heaven to come down to earth. This verse tells us the position God's rule, His kingdom, is to have in our lives on this planet. His will is to be done here just as it is perfectly done in heaven.

The principle Jesus is teaching about prayer is this: We are to start with worship. This puts God first, where He belongs!

I LOVE YOU!

After I was married a few months to Margaret, she turned to me one evening and asked, "Do you love me?"

To me, the question came right out of the blue.

"Of course I love you!" I told her.

But why had she asked? Had I been neglecting her? Had I failed— somehow, some way—to communicate that I was as crazy about her as on the day we said "I do"? Her question threw me a little.

As time went by, I learned that my wife, like most wives, simply needs to hear me say "I love you" from time to time. This doesn't mean she's weak or needy. What it means is that as a husband, I need to be communicating worth to my beloved wife. It's the right thing to do. She has the right to expect that. When I proclaim my love for her, I am honoring my covenant to her and demonstrating where my heart is.

Our prayers should begin in the same manner. We should start our conversation with God in worship—in a manner that clearly demonstrates His holiness, majesty, and power.

But why?

Richard Pratt, in his book *Pray with Your Eyes Open,* teaches that our prayers demonstrate what we really believe about God. If we see God as one who is to jump when we say jump, then our prayers become little more than a list of demands, shoved under heaven's door. We treat God as if He were a genie whose bottle we just rubbed, and now we expect Him to grant us our three wishes.

If we start our dialogue with God in worship, it gets our hearts engaged, and our prayers take on an appropriate attitude. We're more inclined to hear what God has to say to us.

Prayer is like approaching a king. You don't simply run into the throne room and start making requests. No, you walk into the king's throne room, head bowed, taking a knee and demonstrating that you understand the difference between you and the king. God deserves our worship. Our worship postures our hearts in reverence and submission.

"Please" Prayer Demonstrates Our Need

Now back to the text. Do you see a change in the prayer between verses 10 and 11? Verse 11 starts with "Give us." We could describe this half of the prayer as the actual requests. Some call this petition.

The general outline for this prayer is that *we start with worship* (verses 9-10) and *then we ask* (verses 11-13). Do you see now that if we begin with worship, honoring God for who He is, our hearts are prepared to ask Him for our needs? This pattern of prayer puts us into the right mind-set to talk to God. We are telling our heavenly Father that He is God and we are not. He is the one who gives, and we are the ones who receive. This demonstrates to both God and to our own hearts that we are dependent on Him.

How many people in how many far away corners of our world have found comfort, help, and hope in these words that have been traditionally known as the Lord's Prayer? It's been prayed by little children, just learning how to shape their words before the heavenly Father. It's been whispered by patients in hospitals, perhaps in great pain or facing serious surgery. It's been uttered by prisoners, locked away in lonely cells or perhaps even facing execution.

These are wonderful, wonderful words—some of the greatest ever captured in the English language or any language.

But the Lord never intended them as a "magic formula" to somehow open the reluctant gates of heaven. God sees our hearts and knows our needs before we even speak them. We don't have to follow the pattern of Matthew 6 every time we pray. But even so, the words are there for us when our hearts are confused and our thoughts are in a jumble. We can begin with the words, "Our Father who is in heaven, hallowed be Your name..." and find ourselves on the right track.

But when we place our requests before the Lord in prayer, what do we ask for?

If I could return to those dueling mental images of the train and the balloon for a moment... If you are a rigid train, you will simply ask God to bless your already determined path—your fixed, self-appointed agenda. You may ask Him to do a couple of menial tasks, such as keeping the tracks clear of debris or delays from road crossings. But as a train, you will never ask Him to change the path you have chosen for yourself. Instead of saying to God, "Your will be done," you will say, "Let my will be done."

But if you are a balloon, you will ask God to daily meet you. "Give me this day my daily bread." Daily means that you are always dependent on God. It means that you check in with His agenda every single day. It means that you need Him to feed you daily; you must consistently go back to Him for sustenance.

Only What You Need When You Need It

Jean Lerroux, a pastor in Louisiana, shared a poignant childhood memory with his congregation. He recalled going to the county fair with his father and watching as his dad bought a big roll of tickets to use for rides and games scattered around the midway.

But he wouldn't simply hand the tickets over to his son.

Why not? Was he being stingy or controlling?

Not at all. His dad simply wanted his son to keep coming back to him. In that way, they could enjoy a little companionship together, enjoy the shared experiences. This dad wanted his son to keep coming back because he loved him.

So it is with God, our Father. As difficult as it may be to conceive at times, He truly *wants* to be with us. He wants us to come to Him consistently, every single day, to get our needs met by Him and Him alone.

If you think about it, the message about forgiveness in verse 12 is similar to needing daily bread. God wants us to keep short accounts with Him and with others. He doesn't want a day to go by without the records being kept straight. Relationship with God means we are up-to-date on our forgiveness with both God and others. In our prayers we are to continually confess our sins to Him, keeping the relationship fresh. A fresh relationship means that we don't simply talk to God every now and then or only when we find ourselves in trouble and need to place an emergency call to Him. Fresh means that we commune with Him—that we talk to Him often—touching base throughout the day.

Yes, He is there and standing by when we need to make a 9-1-1 call to heaven.

But He's also there to simply talk...even about the smallest details of our day.

A "fresh" relationship with the Lord means we are more like a balloon, willing to be blown by His Spirit wherever, whenever, and however.

Finally, the prayer ends with a request for protection. Remember my rote prayer to "keep my girls safe"? This is not what Jesus is teaching. He is not teaching us that we will always be comfortable and safe. Instead, verse 13 teaches us that we need His help and His protection from both ourselves and the enemy. We need God to protect us from temptation—the evil desires that creep up in our minds. But we also need God to protect us from the evil that comes from our dangerous and tireless adversary, Satan himself.

JOURNEY OF PRAYER

Oh, my friend, there is so much more we could learn about prayer! We have only scratched the surface today on this enormously rich subject. We encourage you to study prayer more in-depth with us by using the book *Lord, Teach Me to Pray in 28 Days*. This book will take you by the hand (just as we seek to do in these pages) and show you how to deepen your relationship with God through prayer.

Spiritual growth is a journey, not some kind of rigid formula. God will take you on different paths at different times of your life to grow you stronger.

But there's another topic in Matthew 6 that (at first) may not seem to have much to do with prayer at all. What is the relationship between prayer and *fasting*? Let's take a closer look.

STARVING TO PRAY

Fasting is setting aside time and food to talk and listen to God. Throughout the Old and New Testaments, we read about God's people fasting. They fasted for various reasons—confession of sins, calling for repentance, seeking help from God in times of great trouble, selecting and ordaining ministers of the gospel, and simply trying to discern God's will for a specific situation. Sometimes fasting was private and sometimes it was corporate. We see corporate and regular fasting in Zechariah 8:19: "Thus says the LORD of hosts, 'The fast of the fourth, the fast of the fifth, the fast of the seventh and the fast of the tenth months will become joy, gladness, and cheerful feasts for the house of Judah; so love truth and peace.'"

The act of going for a time without food, and sometimes drink, has a way of sharpening our focus on God as our sole provider. There have been times in my life when I committed to regularly fast and pray. Times of fasting can be—believe it or not—times of growth. Isn't that backward? To do without is to gain?

Let's look at one passage on prayer and fasting. Read Matthew 6:5-6,16-17. Mark every mention of *prayer* and every mention of *fasting*.

> 5 "When you pray, you are not to be like the hypocrites;
>
> for they love to stand and pray in the synagogues and
>
> on the street corners so that they may be seen by men.
>
> Truly I say to you, they have their reward in full.

6 "But you, when you pray, go into your inner room, close your door and pray to your Father who is in secret, and your Father who sees what is done in secret will reward you."

16 "Whenever you fast, do not put on a gloomy face as the hypocrites do, for they neglect their appearance so that they will be noticed by men when they are fasting. Truly I say to you, they have their reward in full.

17 "But you, when you fast, anoint your head and wash your face."

What do you learn about prayer and fasting in this passage?

KAY'S STORY ON FASTING

My mother, Kay Arthur, tells the story from years ago of receiving an urgent call from Bill Bright, the founder and president of Campus Crusade for Christ.

"Bill Bright...was calling a group of people to join him in prayer and fasting for revival in the United States of America. He had just come off a 40-day fast, and this was God's marching order to this faithful servant of God. That was the beginning of a number of years when we gathered together corporately to fast and pray. Did we see revival? Not really. But God worked in our hearts—and I believe He used those intense, focused times of prayer to restrain evil in our nation.

"I know that one of the primary outcomes of fasting is personal purification. Once when I was fasting because of what I perceived to be a bad attitude in a relationship between people very dear to me, God unexpectedly showed me sin *in my own life*."

A WORD OF CAUTION

I was mentored as a new Christian by reading the biographies of great saints of old. Fasting was a discipline practiced by many of them. And many times it was the discipline that wrought a change, a miracle, a movement...or broke the power of the evil one. The health of some, however, was broken by too much fasting—or fasting for overextended periods of time. Some were greatly weakened, became ill, and had their lives shortened.

I know when I fasted for quite an extended time, I didn't heal from my foot surgery as well as I did when the same surgery was done on the other foot. To me, personally, this was a caution from the Lord. We should make sure to fast as God leads, not because we're simply following the lead or the convictions of others. I don't believe there is anything necessarily sacred about 40 days. When you study everything God teaches on fasting in His Word, you learn that He leads in various types of fasts and for differing periods of time.

So dig into God's Word, do our 40-Minute Bible Study on the subject,[1] learn about this powerful discipline, and let the Lord lead you. Just remember, it's for God, not man.

I can't help but wonder what would happen in America if the leaders of our country called us as a nation to fast, even as the king of Nineveh did in the days of Jonah. Would it break the awful stronghold of iniquity in our nation?

TAKE AWAY

Did you know that Psalm 22:3 tells us that God "inhabits" the praises of His people (KJV)? That is where God is enthroned, where He dwells. Since that is where God is, why don't you try beginning each day with praise? Think about who God is, what He has created, what He has done, what He will do, what He has promised—and praise Him for at least one specific thing.

Listen to Psalm 100:4-5:

> Enter His gates with thanksgiving
> And His courts with praise.
> Give thanks to Him, bless His name.
> For the LORD is good;
> His lovingkindness is everlasting
> And His faithfulness to all generations.

We believe that if you will make this a habit for the remaining days of this study, you will find yourself growing ever stronger in your relationship with your heavenly Father.

Doesn't My Past Mess Everything Up?
Am I Doomed?

KAY

Hello, Beloved of God. It's my turn to take the writer's seat, and I want to begin with a direct, personal question: *Does your past so trouble and shame you that you despair of being used of God in a significant way?*

Maybe you feel like a second-class citizen in the kingdom of God...like you can never be the strong Christian you want to be because of what you were or what you did or even what was done to you. Or maybe you have a friend who feels that way.

If so, do you wonder why God didn't save you—or your child or friend—sooner?

I understand. Let me tell you why. It will take a few minutes, but I think the time will be worth your investment. Besides, if you don't know me, the next few pages will help us to become better acquainted.

Unlike David, I wasn't raised in an evangelical environment. Oh, we went to church; it was part of our culture. I think I can honestly say that it was important to my mom and dad, and it was certainly a part of our regular weekly routine. Always a people person, I loved the church picnics, outings, and youth group. If you had asked me in those years if I was a Christian, I would have said yes.

Wasn't it a given? I was "made in America" and I went to church. Of course I was a Christian!

A DIFFERENT BRAND OF CHRISTIANITY
Our brand of Christianity, however, wasn't about a personal

relationship with Jesus Christ that spilled over into every aspect of life. We never talked about the need to become a child of God, or if we truly believed in Jesus Christ. Ours was more of a "religion" than a personal relationship. I was taught to be good, not holy.

I knew the commandments—or many of them. And I believed that Jesus had died on the cross. A large crucifix in some of the churches testified to that fact, as did the crucifix carried down the aisle Sunday morning by one of the acolytes. I bowed my head when it passed by my pew. I knew when to bow, when to kneel, when to stand, and where the order of service was found in the prayer book. I had been baptized and confirmed. I could recite the Lord's Prayer and the Apostle's Creed, and at the same time check out the congregation. Looking, of course, for the boys!

In general I enjoyed my religion. It was pleasant, fun, wholesome, and in no way interfered with who I was or what I wanted. I thought I was pretty good—and at one point in my young adulthood, I thought God was pretty lucky to have me on His team. Oh, I had immoral thoughts, fantasies about boys, but I was a "good" girl.

I had good parents who had a good marriage, and I wanted one like theirs—maybe with a little "Hollywood" thrown in to spice it up a bit. I grew up, went to Saint Luke's School of Nursing, got my RN, and got married. Although I had plenty of sensual thoughts, I was physically a virgin, saving myself for the man who was to be my husband until we died.

His name was Frank Thomas Goetz Jr., and he went by Tom.

On the inside of my platinum wedding band was "OLIE," which meant, "Our love is eternal." That eternal love lasted six years and produced two sons: Tom and Mark.

I Was Determined to Find Love

Disillusioned and disappointed after our divorce, I determined I would move on. I would find love again. I would not give up my dream of a man who would love me—whether I was pretty or ugly, sick or well, in a good mood or a bad mood. In other words, a man who would love me *unconditionally*.

I moved with my two boys back to the Alexandria/Arlington area of Virginia where we had lived when Tom was in seminary, stood in the living room of our rented apartment, and literally shook my fist in the face of God. "To hell with You, God. I'm going to find someone to love me."

Little did I realize that was precisely what God *had* done—Jesus took my hell because He loved me. He paid the wages of my sin so I could be set free. And he did it all because He loved me—just the way I was!

Eventually I found myself becoming what I thought I would never become—an immoral woman. I had never, never intended to sleep with any man that I didn't marry first. And of course, being a woman of principle, I would never date a married man.

But with sin, you really never say never.

Sin will take you *farther* than you ever wanted to go, keep you *longer* than you ever intended to stay, and *cost* you more than you ever expected to pay.

The man I finally fell deeply in love with turned out to be married. His wife was pregnant with their sixth child. I didn't know it when I met him—I assumed he was single. And when I found out otherwise, I loved him sooo much that I didn't care. The affair lasted two years.

It ended, because in the grace of God, I finally began to feel guilty. With the guilt came resolve: *I'm going to change. I'm not going to do that anymore.* But I did. The good I wanted to do, I couldn't. And the evil I didn't want to do, I did. I thought, *I'm sick, but there's no cure for my sickness because it's not physical.*

THE REST OF THE STORY

The story is too long to tell (it's on CD), but God brought me to my knees. My cry was one of surrender: "God, You can do anything You want to do...I'll never see another man as long as I live...You can paralyze me from the neck down…You can have my two boys… if You'll just give me peace." It was there, on my knees beside my bed, that God saved me.

I remember calling my mother soon after that moment to wish her a happy birthday and to tell her that everything was going to be all right. And somehow I knew it was more than just words. It *would* be all right. My life *had* changed..

At that point, I didn't realize that God had saved me. The word "saved" wasn't even in my vocabulary, nor the vocabulary of the denomination I grew up in. I had never heard someone "give a testimony." What I did know that day was that I belonged to Jesus. When I got up from my knees, I felt like a virgin. I knew that wherever I went, from that time forward and forever, Jesus was going with me. And because of that, I knew I couldn't dress like I'd been dressing or live the way I'd been living.

What had happened to me? The Bible explains it: I was *born again*, as Jesus says in John 3. I was *a new creation* in Christ Jesus, as Paul writes in 2 Corinthians 5:17. The Holy Spirit had moved in, taking up residence in my body, as Jesus promised in John 7:37-39. I was finally able to say *no* to my desires—not that I always did, but I had the power to. I was no longer a slave to my desires, and my desires changed. I wanted to talk about God, to hang out with others who loved Him and knew His Word. I loved the Bible; I couldn't believe I had once thought it boring.

One by one things began to change—my vocabulary, my temper, my desires. Eventually I put down my cigarettes. Nobody told me I should or shouldn't smoke, but God made it clear one night that it wasn't for me. I told Him I couldn't quit. I had tried, and He would just have to do it.

And just like that, He did.

I even came to the point where I told God I was willing to go back to my husband. But before I could tell Tom that, he committed suicide.

Hope of Glory

Oh, there's so much I could share, beloved brother or sister, and maybe someday I will have that opportunity. But you have your own story to tell! Our testimonies of the Lord's grace and working in our lives may be quite different, yet there is a common theme: the delight and power and wonder of His redeeming love. Yes, our stories are different, yet God is working in the life of every true believer in Jesus Christ. The Father, Son, and Spirit, the triune God whom David talked about, now dwells within. Oh, the mystery and wonder of it all: Christ *in* you, the hope of glory.

Read aloud the words of Colossians 1:26-27:

> 26 that is, the mystery which has been hidden from the
> past ages and generations, but has now been mani-
> fested to His saints,

> 27 to whom God willed to make known what is the
> riches of the glory of this mystery among the Gentiles,
> which is Christ in you, the hope of glory.

What's the mystery? Mark it with a blue cloud like this: ⬭. See what the text says and write down what it says.

And whom is it manifested to?

Where is Christ?

What does this guarantee you?

Did you get it? If not, it's okay. Read it again.

The awesome, incredible mystery is that Jesus Christ, Messiah, the anointed promised One, would dwell in us—pitch His tent in the center of our being! That we become "saints"—set apart for God! Belonging to God! Dedicated to God! Consecrated to God!

Truth Worth Relishing

This is mind-boggling, wondrous good news—absolute, pure, and unchangeable! Let it sink in. Savor it. Relish it. It's truth. God said it, had it written down, and then preserved it through the millennia in His book, the Bible. And now He wants you to know it and live accordingly. Knowing this puts a whole new slant on all of life, doesn't it? Your body is His temple, as 1 Corinthians 6:19-20 says.

Jesus told His disciples, "If anyone loves Me, he will keep My word; and My Father will love him, and"—watch it now—"*We will come to him and make Our abode with him*" (John 14:23). We become His home! Our bodies are His temple! I could throw exclamation points all over the page. It is a delightfully divine mystery, isn't it?

Wes King, a Christian artist and friend of ours, wrote a song about this called "Home Inside of Me." The song describes a God who is everywhere, and yet, "Of all the places You could be—You chose to make your home inside of me!"

Jesus in you is evidenced by the changed life that comes with it.

God, Why Didn't You Save Me Sooner?

But let's go back to thoughts that can trouble your mind, such as *Why didn't God save me sooner? I am so ashamed of my past. How can I ever hope to be used of God? I'll always have to sit on the back pew. I'll never be anything but a second-class citizen in the kingdom of God.*

Ever felt that way?

Let me share with you another part of my story and use it for a launching pad into a strong truth that has helped not only me but people with a regretful past like mine be spiritually stronger.

A New Husband and a Dream Realized...in Mexico

As I told you, my first husband committed suicide after I was saved. So, through a set of divinely orchestrated circumstances, I moved from Baltimore, Maryland, to Chattanooga, Tennessee, where I went to Tennessee Temple, the school my second husband graduated from. It's a story I won't go into, but as I prayed for a husband, God showed me I was going to marry Jack Arthur.

And it happened. That's how I knew it was God. Jack showed up on the campus of his alma mater the evening God closed the Diagnostic Hospital where I worked. It was the first and only time they closed it while I worked there. That evening God brought Jack and me face-to-face with each other over two chocolate ice cream cones I had just bought for my boys. My dream was fulfilled, and I ended up right where I longed to be—as a missionary, serving God. We moved to Guadalajara, Mexico.

David was born in Mexico. I didn't know anything about spiritual gifts at the time, but I began exercising my spiritual gift of teaching. I was teaching the teens of the missionaries and their friends and loving every minute of it...except for one thing. I was jealous—jealous of the teens I was teaching.

O God, where were You when I was a teenager? I asked one afternoon. *Why couldn't I have heard these truths when I was young? Why didn't You save me earlier? Why did my sons have to suffer because of me? Why couldn't I have been married to one man, never divorced, never immoral?*

I knew that if God had saved me earlier, I wouldn't have fallen into the sins that had brought so much grief and regret into my life. I was teaching in the book of Romans at that time, learning that salvation not only takes care of the penalty of sin, it breaks the power of sin. As I taught those life-changing precepts from Romans 6–8, I tried to make clear to those young men and women that our identification with Christ in His death, burial, and resurrection—and the gift of His indwelling Spirit—brings us freedom from sin's dominion.

It is wonderful truth, but in that season of my life I actually found myself becoming upset with God and envious of those teens I was teaching. If they listened—if they believed and grabbed hold of these truths—they would never experience the terrible consequences of sin that I had experienced.

And then God spoke to my heart—so very clearly—these words: *I saved you when I wanted to save you. And if you will quit moaning and groaning over it and will share it with others, I will use it.*

A Past Redeemed

All of a sudden I saw how God could redeem a past not lived for Him. It was a lousy past, but if God could use it, then all was not lost and useless. As time went on, God continued to confirm this encouraging perspective through His Word. It was as though He was stringing pearls of truth together, one by one, as His adornment for my troubled soul. My prayer is that He might do the same for you, beloved of God.

The Apostle Paul's Story

The affirmation of the timing of my conversation with God began when I read Galatians 1:15-16, where the apostle Paul refers to his own salvation experience. Because of the complexity of the sentence structure, you might easily miss this pearl. So here is a simple word of advice: read the verses aloud and s-l-o-w-l-y. Watch the commas. Then I'll share what to do next.

> 15 But when God, who had set me apart even from my
>
> mother's womb and called me through His grace, was
>
> pleased

16 to reveal His Son in me so that I might preach Him among the Gentiles, I did not immediately consult with flesh and blood.

Read the verses again. I suggest you color-code the references to *God*, including pronouns, in yellow and the references to *Paul* (the *me, my*) in blue, or put a triangle over God and underline the references to Paul. Then read it yet again and circle in green anything that indicates time or timing.

Now list below what you learn from marking the references to Paul.

And what do you learn from marking *God*? Some of your insights might seem redundant after listing what you learn about Paul, but make the list anyway. Repetition is a key to learning and retaining truth, as is saying something aloud.

Did you see when Paul came to know the Lord? If so, write it out. If not, don't be discouraged. You will.

Now let's leave Galatians for a minute and see what Paul did *before* God revealed His Son in him—or to put it another way, what Paul's life was like before he became a Christian. How does Paul describe himself in the following verse, 1 Timothy 1:15? Read it and underline your insight.

> It is a trustworthy statement, deserving full accep-
> tance, that Christ Jesus came into the world to save
> sinners, among whom I am foremost of all.

What did Paul do that would cause him to describe himself this way—as the foremost, the chief, of sinners?

Acts 6–9 introduces us to Saul, who is later called Paul in the Scriptures. Luke, the author of Acts, introduces us to Saul through the story, message, and martyrdom of a man named Stephen. Stephen had been chosen with six others to help the apostles in caring for the believers; he was "of good reputation, full of the Spirit and of wisdom." Stephen's godliness and courage, however, eventually led to his death at the hands of his fellow Jews. You can read about it in Acts 6 and 7.

As the Jews took Stephen outside the city to stone him because of his convicting message, God lets us know "the witnesses laid aside their robes at the feet of a young man named Saul" (Acts 7:58). This is the first mention of Saul/Paul.

But God doesn't stop there. God wants you to know more about this man who would later identify himself as "the foremost of sinners." He's a key player in the kingdom of God. Read…listen….hear what God wants you to know. As you read, either color the references to *Saul* in blue or underline them.

It's a long passage, but awesome. Besides, these are God's Words—spirit and life, the very bread by which we live. Surely they are better than my words or any human being's words, aren't they? God's Word has no error and is not constrained by the limits of humanity. These words are truth, sanctifying truth. How I love to explain the Word with the Word, to illustrate truth with truth. I am constantly in wonder, amazed, awestruck at these 66 books and how they are woven together in such harmony although written over a period of 1400 to 1800 years by more than 40 men from varied walks of life. Oh, Beloved, if you will love the Word of God, if you will honor it for what it is, you will be strong.

Now, let's see what we learn about Saul/Paul. Mark him!

Acts 8:1-3

> 1 Saul was in hearty agreement with putting him to
> death. And on that day a great persecution began
> against the church in Jerusalem, and they were all
> scattered throughout the regions of Judea and Sama-
> ria, except the apostles.
>
> 2 Some devout men buried Stephen, and made loud
> lamentation over him.
>
> 3 But Saul began ravaging the church, entering house
> after house, and dragging off men and women, he
> would put them in prison.

Acts 9:1-22

> 1 Now Saul, still breathing threats and murder against
> the disciples of the Lord, went to the high priest,
>
> 2 and asked for letters from him to the synagogues at
> Damascus, so that if he found any belonging to the
> Way, both men and women, he might bring them
> bound to Jerusalem.
>
> 3 As he was traveling, it happened that he was
> approaching Damascus, and suddenly a light from
> heaven flashed around him;

4 and he fell to the ground and heard a voice saying to him, "Saul, Saul, why are you persecuting Me?"

5 And he said, "Who are You, Lord?" And He said, "I am Jesus whom you are persecuting,

6 but get up and enter the city, and it will be told you what you must do."

7 The men who traveled with him stood speechless, hearing the voice but seeing no one.

8 Saul got up from the ground, and though his eyes were open, he could see nothing; and leading him by the hand, they brought him into Damascus.

9 And he was three days without sight, and neither ate nor drank.

10 Now there was a disciple at Damascus named Ananias; and the Lord said to him in a vision, "Ananias." And he said, "Here I am, Lord."

11 And the Lord said to him, "Get up and go to the street called Straight, and inquire at the house of Judas for a man from Tarsus named Saul, for he is praying,

12 and he has seen in a vision a man named Ananias come in and lay his hands on him, so that he might regain his sight."

13 But Ananias answered, "Lord, I have heard from

many about this man, how much harm he did to Your saints at Jerusalem;

14 and here he has authority from the chief priests to bind all who call on Your name."

15 But the Lord said to him, "Go, for he is a chosen instrument of Mine, to bear My name before the Gentiles and kings and the sons of Israel;

16 for I will show him how much he must suffer for My name's sake."

17 So Ananias departed and entered the house, and after laying his hands on him said, "Brother Saul, the Lord Jesus, who appeared to you on the road by which you were coming, has sent me so that you may regain your sight and be filled with the Holy Spirit."

18 And immediately there fell from his eyes something like scales, and he regained his sight, and he got up and was baptized;

19 and he took food and was strengthened. Now for several days he was with the disciples who were at Damascus,

20 and immediately he began to proclaim Jesus in the synagogues, saying, "He is the Son of God."

21 All those hearing him continued to be amazed,

and were saying, "Is this not he who in Jerusalem destroyed those who called on this name, and who had come here for the purpose of bringing them bound before the chief priests?"

22 But Saul kept increasing in strength and confounding the Jews who lived at Damascus by proving that this Jesus is the Christ.

Ideally, if we were doing a Precept Upon Precept study[2] together (the most disciplined but rewarding of all the types of Bible studies produced by Precept Ministries International), you would list everything you learn from marking the references to Saul/Paul. You can do that on a separate piece of paper, or you can simply look at each marking and take careful note of what we learn about "the foremost of sinners." Whichever you do, don't miss the things about Saul/Paul that would identify him as a major sinner.

One of the truths you don't want to miss is in verse 15. What does God say about Paul in this verse?

GOD'S TIMING IS PERFECT

Paul destroyed Christians. *If* Paul had been saved earlier, he might have come to Stephen's rescue. *If* Paul had been saved earlier, he might have quelled the great persecution that scattered believers. *If* he had been saved earlier, Christians would not have been destroyed by him; they would have lived, not died.

But according to Galatians 1:15-16, why was Paul saved *when* he was saved? When did God reveal His Son in Paul? The answer is in the text. Write out the answer below. Say it aloud, and get it into your heart. It will make you stronger. Truth always strengthens. Truth liberates us.

When was Paul saved? Paul was saved *when it pleased God*! And it didn't please God to save Paul any sooner. God had a plan. Remember Acts 9:15? God told Paul he was a "chosen instrument of Mine, to bear My name before the Gentiles and kings and the sons of Israel."

If this is true of Paul, it's true of you, Beloved. God revealed His Son in you *when it pleased Him*—not when it pleased you. You couldn't have been saved a day earlier. The Great Redeemer has a plan...*for you*. Oh, we have so much to learn this week that will help you be spiritually strong. I've just begun. But this one awesome truth is enough to think about today, tonight, all night!

TAKE AWAY

God is the Author of every story—my story, David's story, the apostle Paul's story...and yours. Why don't you get on your knees and tell God you want to absorb this truth into the core of your being so you can put to rest all the troublesome memories and regrets of the past and get on with the abundant life He has for you.

Me? Chosen by God? When?

KAY

The more you study God's Word for yourself, rather than *just* listening to the preaching and teaching of others, the more you will understand that your salvation is of God.

PAUL'S GRASP OF THE GOSPEL

The New Testament book we call Ephesians was a letter the apostle Paul wrote to a group of people in the city of Ephesus in Asia Minor (present-day Turkey). Paul had stopped there on his third missionary journey, giving them a priceless gift: the gospel of Jesus Christ.

As a new Christian, I remember that "gospel" was a vague term to me, so let me take a moment to explain the word in simple terms: The gospel is the good news about salvation and the forgiveness of sins through the death, burial, and resurrection of God's sinless Son, Jesus Christ.

According to the book of Acts, Paul stayed in Ephesus and taught these new believers for three months (Acts 19:8). There was a synagogue in Ephesus, but it wasn't a Jewish city. It was the city of Diana, a Greek goddess also called Artemis, whose temple and worship sustained the economy of the city. As a result of this all-out idolatry, the city teemed with evil spirits and unbridled immorality. As Paul boldly declared the gospel of Jesus Christ in that dark place, it was a direct challenge to those who created and trafficked in idols. Many people were saved during Paul's brief ministry in the city, but eventually the pressure on the apostle became so great he was forced to leave. As time went by, Paul ended up in a Roman prison for preaching the gospel, and it was from there he wrote to the believers in Ephesus. That's the letter we'll be looking at together in the next few pages.

With our ability for almost instant communication with people around the world, it's hard for us to grasp what this letter meant to that band of Ephesian believers. I'm so glad it was written down and preserved. It's a magnificent New Testament book that will thrill and strengthen our souls. And just as it helped the Ephesians deal with their past, so it will help you deal with the warfare the enemy can bring against you in your mind.

Remember our subject right now is "dealing with the past," so that you can live with victory and joy in the present and look forward to your future in Christ. As you saw yesterday, God saved Paul when it pleased Him—and that milestone event didn't take place until after Paul had been responsible for the death of some of God's children.

Read Ephesians 1:3-4, which is reproduced below. If you will do three things, you'll be thrilled with what you learn:

- Mark every reference to *God* as you have before. I use yellow. Or, if you prefer, draw a triangle around His name.

- Color every reference to *us* and *we* in orange (or underline).

- Put a circle around any reference to *time* (I usually do this in green).

Basically I follow the marking directions in the front of the *New Inductive Study Bible.*

Ephesians 1:3-6

3 Blessed be the God and Father of our Lord Jesus

Christ, who has blessed us with every spiritual blessing in the heavenly places in Christ,

4 just as He chose us in Him before the foundation of
the world, that we would be holy and blameless before
Him. In love

5 He predestined us to adoption as sons through Jesus
Christ to Himself, according to the kind intention of
His will,

6 to the praise of the glory of His grace, which He freely
bestowed on us in the Beloved.

Now list what you learn from marking

GOD	US/WE
	(which means you and me!)

CHOSEN? BY WHOM? WHEN? WHY?

Now think about what you just learned. These are truths that
belong not only to Paul and those in Ephesus who believed the
gospel more than 2000 years ago but also to you and me, right
now! *You*, beloved of God, were chosen by God to be in Christ—to
become a child of God! I want to put it in bold 20-point characters
and highlight it.

And *when* were you chosen? It was *before* the foundation of the world! What does this mean? It means that before God ever created the world and mankind, He knew that mankind would sin (as we see in Genesis 3).

This means, then, that Jesus, who was active in the creation of the world, knew the time would come for Him to become God incarnate ("in the flesh"), born of a virgin, born without sin, so that He might take our sins and the punishment we deserve and lay down His life for us (even when we were enemies of God—helpless, ungodly sinners without hope, as Romans 5:6-10 tells us).

Take a moment and think about these things. Don't be in a hurry. Read Genesis 1:1-26 and know that before those events happened, and God—Father, Son, and Spirit—said, "Let us make man in our image," He planned *your* salvation. Jesus is the Lamb of God slain from the foundation of the world. This is stunning truth.

So what have we learned so far that can help us grow spiritually strong?

First, that God saved you when it pleased Him. The timing was His alone.

Second, God was acting on a choice He made before the foundation of the world. Your choice, your salvation, was the kind intention of His will.

Third, He predestined your adoption into His family because of love. You are loved! Don't ever doubt it (Romans 8:31-39). And don't ever displease your God and Father by doubting it. When you don't take God at His word, it's not pleasing to Him (Hebrews 11:6).

Fourth, your salvation was all grace: "to the glory of His grace which He freely bestowed on us in the Beloved."

That's enough to digest for today. We'll take a good look at "the riches of His grace" tomorrow, because once you understand it, you can leave the past behind and move into the glorious future He has designed for you.

Take Away

Grace is unearned, unmerited favor. You don't deserve it. Paul didn't. I didn't. David didn't. None of us do. Sinners deserve punishment, and yet through Jesus, we get grace! You can't earn grace. You can only accept it by taking God at His word. Grace is a matter of faith. Can you believe that? Why don't you get alone with God and thank Him for His amazing grace. If you know the words to this hymn by John Newton, the former human trafficker, sing it—or pray it. If you can, get on your knees before your amazing God.

What Does Grace Have to Do with Me?

KAY

If you study church history or read the biographies of saints long gone (yet very much alive in heaven), you'll find one common denominator: These men and women knew the salvation that had transformed their lives was all of God. Grace was theirs for the simple act of believing.

This is why you need to look at the role of grace in your salvation, because understanding it helps you deal with the past and move on to the future—a future lived in the power of that grace.[3]

To understand grace, you have to understand how lost you were—and how loving God is. Read Ephesians 2:1-9, which is printed out below. As you read it, do the following:

- Color every reference to *you, we, us* orange as you did before. Or if we haven't persuaded you to use colors yet, underline it for now, and then please break down and get some colors. Color coding really works.
- Color *God* yellow or use your triangle: God
- Put a heart over *love*: Love

As you mark the text, read it aloud. When you're finished, list what you learn from marking *you, we, us*.

Ephesians 2:1-9

1 And you were dead in your trespasses and sins,

2 in which you formerly walked according to the course of this world, according to the prince of the power of the air, of the spirit that is now working in the sons of disobedience.

3 Among them we too all formerly lived in the lusts of our flesh, indulging the desires of the flesh and of the mind, and were by nature children of wrath, even as the rest.

4 But God, being rich in mercy, because of His great love with which He loved us,

5 even when we were dead in our transgressions, made us alive together with Christ (by grace you have been saved),

6 and raised us up with Him, and seated us with Him in the heavenly places in Christ Jesus,

7 so that in the ages to come He might show the surpassing riches of His grace in kindness toward us in Christ Jesus.

8 For by grace you have been saved through faith; and that not of yourselves, it is the gift of God;

9 not as a result of works, so that no one may boast.

What I Learn About Me From Ephesians 2
What I Was Formerly, What God Did, Why He Did It, and How

Read this remarkable text again, and color a blue circle around *grace*—filling it in with yellow. If we were doing a Precept Upon Precept course, we would have you mark *the prince* (of the power of the air) with a red pitchfork, because this is a reference to your archenemy the devil.

What role does grace play in your salvation? Is it determined by your past? Your goodness? Your anything?

How well did Paul understand grace? Oh, Beloved, it was his theme, his song, his message! Remember what Paul was—"the foremost of sinners"! Now read 1 Corinthians 15:3-10. The verse I want us to focus on is verse 10, but I want you to see it in context. To do this, color every reference to *Paul* in blue or in whatever way you want to mark it.

3 For I delivered to you as of first importance what I also received, that Christ died for our sins according to the Scriptures,

4 and that He was buried, and that He was raised on the third day according to the Scriptures,

5 and that He appeared to Cephas, then to the twelve.

6 After that He appeared to more than five hundred brethren at one time, most of whom remain until now, but some have fallen asleep;

7 then He appeared to James, then to all the apostles;

8 and last of all, as to one untimely born, He appeared to me also.

9 For I am the least of the apostles, and not fit to be called an apostle, because I persecuted the church of God.

10 But by the grace of God I am what I am, and His grace toward me did not prove vain; but I labored even more than all of them, yet not I, but the grace of God with me.

THE PAST IS PAST

Now, what do you learn from this passage about Paul and the grace of God? List it, making sure you take note of what God's grace covered—and what that grace meant to Paul.

In Paul's letter to the church in Philippi, he gives us further inside information regarding who he was before he was saved. Reading this letter, we gain insight into the apostle's all-consuming desire to know Jesus experientially and to be found in Him, not having a righteousness of his own. We encounter his passion for total identification with Jesus' resurrection power. As Paul writes this (and you need to read Philippians 3:1-14 for yourself when you have time), he talks about "the one thing I do." What is that "one thing"? It's what you and I need to do in order to be spiritually strong in His grace. Let me put it in Paul's words: "Forgetting what lies behind and reaching forward to what lies ahead, I press on toward the goal for the prize of the upward call of God in Christ Jesus" (3:13-14).

Oh, Beloved of God, how I wish I could teach this to you face-to-face, to dialogue together. However, I can tell you on the authority of God's Word, your past is past. This is the *first* of four points that will greatly strengthen your walk with the Lord as you remember and consider them. Think about it. The past can never be changed, altered, or rewritten. You can't change it and God won't! God made the past *past* the moment He took you out of the kingdom of darkness and the power of Satan and moved you from death to life into the kingdom of God.

GOD WILL USE YOUR PAST

The *second* point is this: God doesn't change the past, but He does use it. According to all we have learned and the truth of Romans 8:28-31, God uses *your* past (and everything that happens in your future) to conform *you* to the image of His Son. Read it aloud. Using the same system, mark the references to *God* and to those who love Him.

Romans 8:28-31

28 And we know that God causes all things to work together for good to those who love God, to those who are called according to His purpose.

29 For those whom He foreknew, He also predestined to become conformed to the image of His Son, so that He would be the firstborn among many brethren;

30 and these whom He predestined, He also called; and these whom He called, He also justified; and these whom He justified, He also glorified.

31 What then shall we say to these things? If God is for us, who is against us?

God Is Sovereign over Your Past

The *third* point is: God is sovereign, and therefore He is sovereign over your past. No single truth has sustained me more than knowing who God is and understanding that He is sovereign. God rules over all. And if this is true, God is sovereign over your past. Not only did He choose you before the foundation of the world, He formed you (DNA'd you!) in your mother's womb. He chose the egg and the sperm. God created you, designed you, and numbered your days before you ever came to be. This is what Psalm 139:13-16 teaches you.

God Has a Purpose

Fourth and finally, there is purpose in your life—past, present, and future. It is God's purpose, and He is a God of purpose. I love the phrase "according to His purpose who works all things after the counsel of His will" (Ephesians 1:11).

Take Away

Have I worn you out? I pray not. Now you must think on these things, dear brother, dear sister. One light reading won't do it. Go over what you've seen. Mark these Scriptures in your Bible. And when the past rears its ugly head, drop the plumb line of these truths against it and believe God. It will bring peace.

Explain to Me Unconditional Love

KAY

Oh, the security of knowing you are loved with an everlasting love! Remember in my testimony how I told you I shook my fist in the face of God and said, "To hell with You, God. I'm going to find someone to love me"?

When I did that, do you imagine God angry or...smiling? From what you've seen these past three days from His Word, you realize that my desire for "someone to love me" unconditionally was what God had in mind for me all the time. And from all time! From the creation of the heavens and the earth. Jesus was the very Man my heart had longed for—a Man who would love me so much He would lay down His life for a wretch like me.

THE TRUTH THAT CHANGES EVERYTHING

I can honestly tell you that since I came to know God through my salvation and through His Word, I have never ever doubted His love. Yes, I know there have been times when I have hurt Him greatly, choosing to disobey Him and yielding instead to the corrupt desires of my heart. And there have also been times when I have felt overwhelmed by disappointment, pain, heartache, and rejection. But even in those times, I never, ever doubted His love.

Knowing that you are loved unconditionally is redemptive. It helps you grow spiritually strong and enables you to love others.

First John 4 tells us God is love. "Love" is used 27 times in verses 7-21. The theme of this chapter is evident, isn't it? Love. Let's look at it for a moment. Remember, His words are life. There's energy in them—transforming power.

How Can I Know That I Am a Christian?

First John is the book that helps you know you truly belong to Him, that you really do have eternal life (5:11-13). All you have to do is read through this short letter and mark the word *know,* and then make a list of WHAT you know and HOW you know it. Then look at how you measure up. It will show you whether you've got the real thing...whether you *are* the real thing—a genuine Christian.

One of the ways you can know you are truly His child and have eternal life is that you love God's children. We'll go into that tomorrow. Today, I want you to see why you are loved. How you can be sure. So read the following verses, and mark the references to *God* as you've been doing, and put a heart over every occurrence of *love*.

1 John 4:7-10

> 7 Beloved, let us love one another, for love is from God;
>
> and everyone who loves is born of God and knows God.
>
> 8 The one who does not love does not know God, for
>
> God is love.
>
> 9 By this the love of God was manifested in us, that God
>
> has sent His only begotten Son into the world so that
>
> we might live through Him.
>
> 10 In this is love, not that we loved God, but that He
>
> loved us and sent His Son to be the propitiation for
>
> our sins.

Now list what you learn from marking the references to God. Don't miss a one.

Good… But there's more I want you to see in 1 John 4. This time as you read the text that follows, mark (or color orange) every *we, us, one, him*—and then again mark *love* with a heart.

1 John 4:16-18

> 16 We have come to know and have believed the love
>   which God has for us. God is love, and the one who
>   abides in love abides in God, and God abides in him.
>
> 17 By this, love is perfected with us, so that we may have
>   confidence in the day of judgment; because as He is,
>   so also are we in this world.
>
> 18 There is no fear in love; but perfect love casts out fear,
>   because fear involves punishment, and the one who
>   fears is not perfected in love.

Now list what you learn from marking *we, us, one, him*. It will really encourage you to see this list, so read it through after you record it.

Now stop and think about what you have learned from simply marking these two sets of verses. God is love. God first loved you—not you Him! God expressed His love, demonstrated His love, proved His love, and validated that He is love by sending His Son for you when you didn't even love Him. Jesus came to be the propitiation for your sins.

Heavy Theology? Or Beauty Set to Words?

"Propitiation" is a big word.

But oh, my friend, it's also radiantly, unspeakably beautiful.

Every child of God needs to know and understand that propitiation, in essence, means "satisfaction." It's a word that goes all the way back to the Torah—the first five books of the Bible. If you ever do our Romans Precept course, you'll really get the theological picture. Romans is the constitution of our faith, a book we all need to know firsthand, and David's favorite New Testament book.

For now, however, "propitiation" means that God's holiness, righteousness, and justice were totally satisfied by the sacrifice of the Messiah, Christ Jesus. Therefore *your* sins—past, present, and future—could be justly and righteously forgiven through Jesus' shed blood. Apart from the shedding of blood, there is no forgiveness of sins; yet the blood of bulls and goats (animal sacrifices) could never take away man's sin. Only the untainted, spotless blood of a sinless man could do it, and there has been only one of those: Jesus Christ, the Son of God, the Son of man.

This means that God's love covers your sin. It's not an excuse for sin—and if you are truly born into God's family, sin is no longer the habit of your life. First John 3:4-10 makes that clear. When you do sin, however, God in His great love provides you with an advocate—a person to stand beside you, plead your case, and come to your defense. Listen to 1 John 2:1-2. As you read it, mark every reference to *Jesus* including any synonyms.

1 John 2:1-2

> 1 My little children, I am writing these things to you so that you may not sin. And if anyone sins, we have an Advocate with the Father, Jesus Christ the righteous;
>
> 2 and He Himself is the propitiation for our sins; and

not for ours only, but also for those of the whole world.

How is Jesus described in these verses, and what do you learn from marking the references to Him?

WHO HAS YOUR BACK?

When it says Jesus is our Advocate, you will note He is the advocate of those who are His children, who have God as their Father. When God tells you Jesus is the propitiation for your sins, He also lets you know Jesus died for the sins of the whole world, not just those who would believe on Him. Those in the world *could* be God's children if they would believe on Jesus Christ; Jesus died for their sins also. But they refuse to believe, and disbelief is the sin that consigns people to the lake of fire forever.

An advocate is like a lawyer, one who pleads your case. The word in the Greek is *paraklētas*, one who is called alongside to help another, an intercessor. Remember when David taught you about the Spirit? *Paraklētas* is the word used also of the Spirit, the Helper, who comes to indwell us.

Goodness! You have all sorts of assurances of His everlasting love, don't you? God is love. The Father, Son, and Holy Spirit abide in you. God is eternal, and in Him you have eternal life. God promises He will never leave nor forsake you (Hebrews 13:5-6).

Do you see, my friend, "how great a love the Father has bestowed on us, that we would be called children of God; and such we are" (1 John 3:1)?

So how does all this play out practically and make us spiritually strong? I think God says it better than I can. Read the following passage from Romans. Since it's for you, mark *we, us, elect* in orange, and mark the references to *love* with a heart.

Romans 8:31–39

31 What then shall we say to these things? If God is for us, who is against us?

32 He who did not spare His own Son, but delivered Him over for us all, how will He not also with Him freely give us all things?

33 Who will bring a charge against God's elect? God is the one who justifies;

34 who is the one who condemns? Christ Jesus is He who died, yes, rather who was raised, who is at the right hand of God, who also intercedes for us.

35 Who will separate us from the love of Christ? Will tribulation, or distress, or persecution, or famine, or nakedness, or peril, or sword?

36 Just as it is written,

"FOR YOUR SAKE WE ARE BEING PUT TO DEATH ALL DAY LONG; WE WERE CONSIDERED AS SHEEP TO BE SLAUGHTERED."

37 But in all these things we overwhelmingly conquer through Him who loved us.

38 For I am convinced that neither death, nor life, nor angels, nor principalities, nor things present, nor things to come, nor powers,

39 nor height, nor depth, nor any other created thing, will be able to separate us from the love of God, which is in Christ Jesus our Lord.

Your last glorious exercise for today is to list what you learned from marking the references to you—*we, us, elect.*

TAKE AWAY

Now, Beloved, do you understand why I call you "beloved"? It's not a feminine term of endearment, nor is it saccharin goosh. It's a word used by Peter, Paul, John, Jude…a word God breathed about you! Remember you *are* beloved.

So what is your prayer? Write it out below. Perhaps what you've learned will stir you to do more than write. Maybe you will be inspired to create a poem, a song, or even a painting. However God leads you to respond, share your expression with others so they can be blessed too.

How Am I to Love Others? And Why?

KAY

Loving others with the love of God will help you grow spiritually strong.

I truly love loving others, and when I do, I honestly feel that I have pleased my Father. When I fail, however, or when I hear that people don't think I have loved as I ought to, it crushes my spirit. And in those times when I have carelessly or willfully chosen to act in an unloving way, I feel utterly miserable until I've made it right with my God and right with my loved one.

WE NEED TO LOVE—IT'S GOOD FOR US

There has to be some sort of hormone—some endorphic juice—that is secreted through the body when we love. I'm sure that with all the new research on the brain, they will find it. God *designed* us for love: We need it and we need to express it.

Love is a characteristic of the spiritually strong. Galatians 5:22 tells us that when we are filled with the Spirit, it is evidenced in a nine-fold way: love, joy, peace, patience, kindness, goodness, faithfulness, gentleness, and self-control. Did you notice that love is at the head of the list? Some believe that love summarizes the other eight.

A STORY FROM THE HOLOCAUST

A story from Corrie ten Boom's life comes to mind. Let me share it, and then we'll explore the Scriptures to help you know for certain the priority of loving others. At one period in America's history, there was no need to tell you who this Dutch spinster was. (I know "spinster" is an old-fashioned term, but it truly describes what Corrie was like.) Corrie was a sturdy woman, dressed as older women used to dress, with salt-and-pepper hair rolled up in a bun. She wore the fragrance of purity that comes from the innocence of never knowing a man and keeping one's thoughts tuned to God. She was also a no-nonsense woman.

She had an older sister named Betsie who went to one of Hitler's concentration camps with her. Their crime? They, with their godly father, hid Jews in their home during the dark, demonic days of the Holocaust. Both were shamed and mistreated in prison. Betsie died, and Corrie survived only because of a clerical error that allowed her to leave the camp.

After a time, Corrie became what she described as "a tramp for the Lord," traveling the world—and eventually Germany—telling of the unfailing, all-sufficient love of God. Going to Germany with this message was incredibly hard on Corrie, for this was the land, the people, of her persecutors. These were the ones who took the life of her father, her beloved nephew, and her Betsie. Yet she told God she would tell of His love and forgiveness wherever He sent her.

Her heavy Dutch accent seemed to give great authority to her proclamation, "God is willing to forgive us our sins. There is no one beyond His love."

Following one of her speaking engagements, a crowd, as usual, gathered about this woman of God. Her habit was to receive the words of kindness and praise as one would receive flowers from admirers, and then at night, before she closed her eyes for sleep, she would hand the bouquet to her Lord.

But this night there was no thought of flowers, for thrust in front of her was the yet strong hand of the German prison guard who had mercilessly beat her Betsie before her eyes. She herself had been abused by this man. She could have handled that. But after what he had done to Betsie...?

For a moment Corrie stared at the man's hand as his words bombarded her heart: "I am so glad to know that God can forgive anyone for what they have done." His hand was suspended in air as Corrie raised her eyes, looked at the dreaded face, and cried in her heart, "O Gott, I cannot forgive this man. I cannot love him. But in obedience to You, I will take his hand."*

When her fingers touched his, Corrie felt the love of God flow from her to her persecutor. That night, the bouquet offered to God was not flowers from others, but one Corrie had picked herself. She experienced a new depth of strength in her life because she had walked in love just as Christ had loved her and gave Himself up for her (Ephesians 5:1).

WHAT KIND OF LOVE MAKES US SPIRITUALLY STRONG?

Let's take a look at this loving that makes us spiritually strong. We'll begin by returning to 1 John, the New Testament letter that tells you how you can *know* that you have eternal life. And why is this so important? I think you know, don't you? You can't love others in the way you should or with the quality of love they need if you don't first have that love in yourself. Read the following verses and put a heart over the references to *love*. I mark *hate* with a black heart.

1 John 3:10-11

> 10 By this the children of God and the children of the
>
> devil are obvious: anyone who does not practice righ-
>
> teousness is not of God, nor the one who does not love
>
> his brother.

---

* I am quoting Corrie as best as I can remember her. These are not her exact words, but in essence they say what I heard years ago when I listened to a cassette tape of her message to a church. I was so touched by this woman's life and story, and I have read most of her writings. You might want to get the wonderful movie *The Hiding Place*. My dear friend Jeannette Cliff George plays the role of Corrie.

11 For this is the message which you have heard from the beginning, that we should love one another;

1 John 3:14-18

14 We know that we have passed out of death into life, because we love the brethren. He who does not love abides in death.

15 Everyone who hates his brother is a murderer; and you know that no murderer has eternal life abiding in him.

16 We know love by this, that He laid down His life for us; and we ought to lay down our lives for the brethren.

17 But whoever has the world's goods, and sees his brother in need and closes his heart against him, how does the love of God abide in him?

18 Little children, let us not love with word or with tongue, but in deed and truth.

1 John 3:23

23 This is His commandment, that we believe in the name of His Son Jesus Christ, and love one another, just as He commanded us.

1 John 4:20–21

> 20 If someone says, "I love God," and hates his brother, he is a liar; for the one who does not love his brother whom he has seen, cannot love God whom he has not seen.

> 21 And this commandment we have from Him, that the one who loves God should love his brother also.

1 John 5:1-2

> 1 Whoever believes that Jesus is the Christ is born of God, and whoever loves the Father loves the child born of Him.

> 2 By this we know that we love the children of God, when we love God and observe His commandments.

Now, once again, look at every place you marked *love* and list what you learn from the Word of God about loving others. As you make the list, watch also for how love is to be expressed.

BOTTOM LINE

So what's the bottom line?
No love, no Jesus.
No love, no salvation.

Love is the outcome of salvation, the evidence that God—who is love—dwells in you. If you love, then you will automatically fulfill the law, the commandments of God. Listen to what Jesus said when a scribe (a copier and interpreter of the law) asked Jesus an important question:

Matthew 22:36-40

> 36 "Teacher, which is the great commandment in the Law?"
>
> 37 And He said to him, "'You shall love the Lord your God with all your heart, and with all your soul, and with all your mind.'
>
> 38 "This is the great and foremost commandment.
>
> 39 "The second is like it, 'You shall love your neighbor as yourself.'
>
> 40 "On these two commandments depend the whole Law and the Prophets."

Why don't you read it one more time aloud and mark two things: *love* and *commandment* (you could mark *commandment* like this).

So what do you learn about love? Who are you to love? Why are you to love them?

If love can be commanded, what does that tell you about it?

Can a child of God love like this? How do you know? As you answer, draw from everything you've seen in the Word of God these past two days.

Before we let the apostle Paul press us hard on the practicalities or the outworking of love toward others, I want us to see what Jesus said to His disciples in the upper room. He said it after He washed their feet and they ate the Passover meal, at which He inaugurated the new covenant in His blood. Once again mark the references to *love* with a heart and color *you* and *one another* orange.

John 13:34-35

> 34 "A new commandment I give to you, that you love one
>   another, even as I have loved you, that you also love
>   one another.
> 35 "By this all men will know that you are My disciples,
>   if you have love for one another."

So what do you learn?

I have to admit I would read this passage and, instead of hanging on God's every word, I just focused on "a new commandment." I remember thinking to myself, "Why is that new? It's just a fulfill-ment of the Old Testament law. There's nothing new about that." Well, one day when I truly took time to observe the text, valuing and hanging on His every word, I finally got it.

The Old Testament law told us to love our neighbor as we love ourselves. But Jesus said, "Love one another, *even as I have loved you.*" That takes love to a dramatic new level. Oh, to be so filled with the Spirit that I would at all times love others as Jesus loved them. Doesn't it just make you want to stop and pray about it right now? It does me. Shall we pray together?

YOU CALLED ME "BELOVED"

O Father, I am so convicted because I don't always love others this way. I get so busy, in such a hurry I forget my redemption is all about love. Your love for me. Your unconditional, merciful love that saw my need and moved beyond who I was and what I had done. You called me "beloved" when there was nothing lovely about me. O Father, thank You, thank You, thank You. And thank You, Jesus, that although You despised the shame of the cross and the rejection that came with it, You said, "Not My will, but Yours be done." Now please remind me to love with Your love, to walk by the Spirit, to love as You loved—seeking only Your will, desiring only to behave, respond, and act in such a way that it shows You all are in me. Please, please make me instantly aware when I'm off course.

Now then, let's go to Ephesians 4, the chapter in Paul's letter that moves from what I'll call the doctrinal—the teaching of what it means to be *in Christ* and thus part of His body, the church—to the practical outworking of it all. After Paul tells us in Ephesians 2 how we formerly walked (we looked at this earlier), in Ephesians 4 and 5 he tells us how we are *now* to walk. We are to:

- 4:1—walk in a manner worthy of the calling with which we've been called

- 4:17—walk no longer as the Gentiles do in the futility of their darkened minds
- 5:1—walk in love just as Christ also loved us and gave Himself up for us
- 5:8—walk as children of light
- 5:15—not walk as unwise men but as wise, making the most of our time...as we keep on being filled with the Spirit (5:18)

In Ephesians 4:25–5:2, we see how this walk causes us to interface with others, how our love of God manifests itself in loving others. As you read it, underline every instruction, everything God is telling you to do.

Ephesians 4:25–5:2

25 Therefore, laying aside falsehood, speak truth each one of you with his neighbor, for we are members of one another.

26 Be angry, and yet do not sin; do not let the sun go down on your anger,

27 and do not give the devil an opportunity.

28 He who steals must steal no longer; but rather he must labor, performing with his own hands what is good, so that he will have something to share with one who has need.

29 Let no unwholesome word proceed from your mouth, but only such a word as is good for edification

according to the need of the moment, so that it will give grace to those who hear.

30 Do not grieve the Holy Spirit of God, by whom you were sealed for the day of redemption.

31 Let all bitterness and wrath and anger and clamor and slander be put away from you, along with all malice.

32 Be kind to one another, tender-hearted, forgiving each other, just as God in Christ also has forgiven you.

5:1 Therefore be imitators of God, as beloved children;

2 and walk in love, just as Christ also loved you and gave Himself up for us, an offering and a sacrifice to God as a fragrant aroma.

Take Away

Take another look at every instruction that you underlined. Is there anything you're doing that you need to stop doing? If so, either put a star by it or write it below, along with the name of anyone who comes to your mind in respect to that instruction.

It's obedience to the Word of God that makes you spiritually strong. How strong do you want to be? Corrie put her hand out in faith, and God supplied what she needed for the task. Will you do the same? If not, why not? Write it out, and then read it aloud to God and ask Him to show you what He thinks about your reason. He'll answer if you ask.

Is There a Cross in Your Life?

Kay

Anyone who will carefully read the New Testament book of 2 Corinthians will have a deep admiration for the apostle Paul. He was one valiant warrior. God's grace, as he wrote, wasn't poured out on him for nothing! Paul labored more than all the apostles, and yet here's his secret—it wasn't Paul, it was the grace of God working in him.

In this highly personal letter, the apostle bares his heart to the church in Corinth, revealing things about himself that are revealed in no other Scriptures. You'll be blessed and challenged by reading it, and intrigued to find out how he could be so spiritually strong. Remember, as you read, this is the man who wrote in his letter to the Philippians that he had "not attained and was not perfect" but was pressing on (Philippians 4:12).

2 Corinthians 11:23-31

> 23 Are they servants of Christ?—I speak as if insane—I more so; in far more labors, in far more imprisonments, beaten times without number, often in danger of death.

> 24 Five times I received from the Jews thirty-nine lashes.

> 25 Three times I was beaten with rods, once I was stoned, three times I was shipwrecked, a night and a day I have spent in the deep.

26 I have been on frequent journeys, in dangers from rivers, dangers from robbers, dangers from my countrymen, dangers from the Gentiles, dangers in the city, dangers in the wilderness, dangers on the sea, dangers among false brethren;

27 I have been in labor and hardship, through many sleepless nights, in hunger and thirst, often without food, in cold and exposure.

28 Apart from such external things, there is the daily pressure on me of concern for all the churches.

29 Who is weak without my being weak? Who is led into sin without my intense concern?

30 If I have to boast, I will boast of what pertains to my weakness.

31 The God and Father of the Lord Jesus, He who is blessed forever, knows that I am not lying.

REAL PAIN, REAL SUFFERING

There was nothing plastic or artificial about the apostle Paul. And even though there were those in the church at Corinth who mocked him or opposed him, he didn't hold back from declaring to them his experiences—the ups and downs, the highs and lows of his ministry and his walk with Christ. When he was in Macedonia, he told them how he had felt afflicted on every side, assaulted by conflicts without and fears within. And even though he had been used of the Lord to help and encourage so many others across the civilized world, it was a time when he himself felt emotionally low and in need of comfort (2 Corinthians 7:5-6).

Paul was a real, flesh-and-blood man who deeply desired to be pleasing to his God (2 Corinthians 5:9), and tried to avoid saying or doing anything that would cause offense or discredit the ministry

(2 Corinthians 6:3). His desire, with Timothy his son-in-the-Lord, was to commend himself as a servant of God:

> in much endurance, in afflictions, in hardships, in distresses, in beatings, in imprisonments, in tumults, in labors, in sleeplessness, in hunger, in purity, in knowledge, in patience, in kindness, in the Holy Spirit, in genuine love, in the word of truth, in the power of God; by the weapons of righteousness for the right hand and the left, by glory and dishonor, by evil report and good report; regarded as deceivers and yet true; as unknown yet well-known, as dying yet behold, we live; as punished yet not put to death, as sorrowful yet always rejoicing, as poor yet making many rich, as having nothing yet possessing all things (2 Corinthians 6:4-10).

Does it make your mouth water? It does mine...and at the same time it greatly convicts me. If I want to live this life, am I willing to pay the price? And what, Beloved, would you say would be the price?

I think it's clear. Jesus didn't mince words with the multitude who were enamored with this One who cast out demons, healed the sick, stopped the wind, and fed the multitudes. As you read the text, mark *anyone* and *whoever* along with the pronouns that go with them. Orange is a good color.

Mark 8:34-38

> 34 And He summoned the crowd with His disciples, and said to them, "If anyone wishes to come after Me, he must deny himself, and take up his cross and follow Me.

35 "For whoever wishes to save his life will lose it, but whoever loses his life for My sake and the gospel's will save it.

36 "For what does it profit a man to gain the whole world, and forfeit his soul?

37 "For what will a man give in exchange for his soul?

38 "For whoever is ashamed of Me and My words in this adulterous and sinful generation, the Son of Man will also be ashamed of him when He comes in the glory of His Father with the holy angels."

Once again, make a list of the insights you get from marking references to those who wish to come after Jesus. When you finish, take a few minutes to consider what you listed.

What do you think about this? How does it hit you?

Do you want to sign up? Or have you?

And what if you don't?

Take Away

What does "following Jesus" look like in your life? Does it include suffering? Pain? Persecution? Could Jesus be serious when He calls His followers to take up their cross? When you read the Gospels, you need to pay close attention to all that Jesus says about what it means to follow Him. Take some time today and ask your heavenly Father to show where you may be missing the cross in your life.

Holiness? For Me?

KAY

I've become a saint."

"You've become a *what*?"

"A saint."

"No way!"

Is that the reaction you would expect from friends if you told them you were now set apart for God?

Even so, the statement is true. If you have found salvation in Jesus Christ, you have been set apart for God, and that is precisely what it means to be a saint. What people don't often know is that the Greek word translated "saints" (*hagioi*) has the same root as holy (*hagios*), and means "one set apart for God."

But what does all this really mean, in practical terms? And what does it have to do with growing spiritually strong? That's what we will be looking at in today's study. Understanding this truth and then pursuing sanctification, holiness, "without which no one will see the Lord" (Hebrews 12:14), will keep you spiritually strong.

Your holiness is the will of God. Listen to 1 Peter 1:14-16: "As obedient children, do not be conformed to the former lusts which were yours in your ignorance, but like the Holy One who called you, be holy yourselves also in all your behavior because it is written, 'You shall be holy, for I am holy.' "

"You shall be holy" is a command from God. It's neither optional nor negotiable. The tense of the verb in Greek tells us this.

So on that note, let's explore the subject of holiness. You'll find it tucked in Scriptures throughout the Old and New Testaments under the words "saints," "sanctify," "sanctified," "sanctification," "consecrate" and "consecration," and of course "holy" and "holiness."

The basic word for holiness in the Old Testament means to "be holy, removed from common use." The main idea is separation from evil to good, from common to holy use. That's a picture of you, when you become God's child. When "holy" words are used in the New Testament, their common Greek root is *hagios*. Saints, then, are holy ones. Watch how the apostle Paul opens the book of Romans: "to all who are beloved of God in Rome, called as saints" (1:7). What a calling!

Libraries of books have been written on the subject of holiness. There is so much to explore, learn, and meditate on. Since our study is confined to 28 days, however, let's get an overview of holiness, the broad picture from the Scriptures. Then, as you study the Bible for yourself, you will have a framework for this vital and sometimes misunderstood subject.

Why is it misunderstood? Because many people today equate the term "holiness" with *legalism*—slavishly following a man-made set of dos and don'ts. That, Beloved, is not holiness. It's not even close! True holiness is rather the living out of what God accomplished for you and in you.

The Who of Holiness

As you just saw in 1 Peter 1:14-16, God is holy, and it is written that we are to be holy as He is holy. Where is it written? The first time God declares His holiness is in the third book of the Bible, Leviticus. Leviticus is the part of the Torah, the first five books of the Bible. The setting of Leviticus, which covers a period of one month, is Mount Sinai, where Moses received the law from God.

In Leviticus 10, God has Moses record a very sobering and critical incident, and it is the introduction to what follows. As you read it, remember Nadab and Abihu, by virtue of being sons of Aaron, are part of the priesthood and therefore have the privilege of entering the holy place and offering incense on the altar. All of this occurs within the tabernacle—the tent of meeting set up according to God's careful pattern—where the nation of Israel would worship the Lord according to His statutes.

As you read the text, mark all references to *the Lord* as you have previously marked *God*. Put a cloud around *holy* and color it yellow.

Leviticus 10:1-11

1 Now Nadab and Abihu, the sons of Aaron, took their respective firepans, and after putting fire in them, placed incense on it and offered strange fire before the LORD, which He had not commanded them.

2 And fire came out from the presence of the LORD and consumed them, and they died before the LORD.

3 Then Moses said to Aaron, "It is what the LORD spoke, saying,

'By those who come near Me I will be treated as holy, And before all the people I will be honored.'"

So Aaron, therefore, kept silent.

4 Moses called also to Mishael and Elzaphan, the sons of Aaron's uncle Uzziel, and said to them, "Come forward, carry your relatives away from the front of the sanctuary to the outside of the camp."

5 So they came forward and carried them still in their tunics to the outside of the camp, as Moses had said.

6 Then Moses said to Aaron and to his sons Eleazar and Ithamar, "Do not uncover your heads nor tear your clothes, so that you will not die and that He will not become wrathful against all the congregation. But your kinsmen, the whole house of Israel, shall bewail the burning which the LORD has brought about.

7 "You shall not even go out from the doorway of the tent of meeting, or you will die; for the LORD's anointing oil is upon you." So they did according to the word of MOSES.

8 THE LORD then spoke to Aaron, saying,

9 "Do not drink wine or strong drink, neither you nor your sons with you, when you come into the tent of meeting, so that you will not die—it is a perpetual statute throughout your generations—

10 and so as to make a distinction between the holy and the profane, and between the unclean and the clean,

11 and so as to teach the sons of Israel all the statutes which the LORD has spoken to them through Moses."

Now, what did you learn from marking the references to the Lord? Write it out.

What a story! The deaths of these two young men, warranted by their arrogant presumption and executed by the Lord Himself, makes His point clear. God intends to be treated as holy, to be honored as God, by those who would come near to Him. There is a way—a proper way—to worship God: *His* way! No wonder Aaron was not allowed to mourn the death of his sons by unbinding his head and tearing his clothes.

Now, move to verse 10. A distinction is to be made between what?

It is in Leviticus 11, as God introduces the difference between the clean and the unclean, that God tells Israel for the *first* time that He is holy. The sanctifier of the Sabbath (Genesis 2:3) and of the ground Moses stood on before the burning bush (Exodus 3:5) wants His people to understand who He is and what they are to be. Read Leviticus 11:44-45. As you do, underline the command to *be holy* and put a cloud around *I am holy* and color it yellow or choose a marking of your design that you can use in your Bible.

Leviticus 11:44-45

> 44 "'For I am the LORD your God. Consecrate yourselves therefore, and be holy; for I am holy. And you shall not make yourselves unclean with any of the swarming things that swarm on the earth.

> 45 'For I am the LORD, who brought you up from the land of Egypt, to be your God; thus you shall be holy for I am holy.'"

Now, stop and look at what you observed from God's Word.

Who is holy?

Why are we to be holy?

Now does that seem reasonable? Of course! God commands it. We were made in the image of God, and yet, in Adam, we sinned. God's image was blurred and distorted, and death came upon all men, for all sinned (Romans 5:12). Yet our great Redeemer is in the business of redemption. He wants His image restored in man whom He created, and He has a way to bring it about.

WHAT IS HOLINESS?

So what is holiness? Holiness is being clean, pure, consecrated, set apart, dedicated to God, and separated from everything unclean. "Blameless," "beyond reproach," and "godliness" are words that accompany holiness, defining it even more.

And who is a saint? A saint is a holy one, a person set apart for God. If that's what "saint" means, then how do you feel about being a saint? And how does that happen?

HOW ON EARTH CAN A PERSON BE HOLY?

Let's fast-forward to the Gospel of Luke to the words of Zacharias, the father of John the Baptist, the forerunner of Jesus. Listen to the words of Zacharias as he prophesied under the filling of the Holy Spirit. Watch for the words "redemption," "salvation," "holiness," and "righteousness." Mark *holiness* as you've marked *holy* previously.

Luke 1:67-75

67 And his father Zacharias was filled with the Holy
Spirit, and prophesied, saying:

68 "Blessed be the Lord God of Israel,

For He has visited us and accomplished redemption
for His people,

69 And has raised up a horn of salvation for us

In the house of David His servant—

70 As He spoke by the mouth of His holy prophets from
of old—

71 Salvation from our enemies,

And from the hand of all who hate us;

72 To show mercy toward our fathers,

And to remember His holy covenant,

73 The oath which He swore to Abraham our father,

74 To grant us that we, being rescued from the hand of
our enemies,

Might serve Him without fear,

75 In holiness and righteousness before Him all our
days."

When you read this passage and pay attention to the words we
had you watch for, you see that redemption and salvation lead to

serving God without fear, in holiness and righteousness before Him all our days.

What a salvation! It is a salvation accomplished by the one and only Savior, Jesus Christ. Look at Hebrews 10:10-14, where the author of Hebrews under the inspiration of the Spirit explains why the old covenant sacrificial system has been replaced by the death of Jesus Christ. Mark *sanctified* as you marked *holy*.

Hebrews 10:10-14

10 By this will we have been sanctified through the offering of the body of Jesus Christ once for all.

11 Every priest stands daily ministering and offering time after time the same sacrifices, which can never take away sins;

12 but He, having offered one sacrifice for sins for all time, sat down at the right hand of God,

13 waiting from that time onward until His enemies be made a footstool for His feet.

14 For by one offering He has perfected for all time those who are sanctified.

SANCTIFIED! WHERE AND HOW?

In the following paragraphs, we're going to get just a little bit technical. But what we're teaching here will have a very practical and encouraging outcome in your life, so please hang in there!

The verb structure of "sanctified" (perfect passive participle) in verse 10 tells us that this is a sanctification that is complete. Done. Which means when you believe in Jesus Christ, you are set apart for

God forever. It's a God-done thing, never to be undone. What confidence and strength that ought to give you. Yet, that's not the end of it. Verse 14 tells us "He has perfected for all time" (again, "perfected" is in the perfect tense, a past completed action with a present result) those who are sanctified ("sanctified" is a present participle, which indicates an ongoing process—*being* sanctified).

That ought to bring a gigantic sigh of relief. Why? Because we know, don't we, that we aren't as holy as we ought to be. There is room for improvement. So how is that improvement made? We'll explore that in a minute.

Before we go any further, we want you to see the work of the Spirit in all this, what this makes you, and how you are to live.

Here's the work of the Spirit: "But we should always give thanks to God for you, brethren beloved by the Lord, because God has chosen you from the beginning for salvation through sanctification by the Spirit and faith in the truth" (2 Thessalonians 2:13). What does the Spirit do? He sanctifies you, sets you apart, makes you holy—a saint, a holy one. Salvation occurs through this sanctifying work of the Holy Spirit and through faith in the truth, the Word of God.

Consequently what do you become? And why? Read 1 Peter 2:9-12 and mark every *you, your,* and *beloved.*

1 Peter 2:9-12

> 9 But you are a chosen race, A royal priesthood, a holy nation, a people for God's own possession, so that you may proclaim the excellencies of Him who has called you out of darkness into His marvelous light;

> 10 for you once were not a people, but now you are the people of God; you had not received mercy, but now you have received mercy.

11 Beloved, I urge you as aliens and strangers to abstain from fleshly lusts which wage war against the soul.

12 Keep your behavior excellent among the Gentiles, so that in the thing in which they slander you as evil-doers, they may because of your good deeds, as they observe them, glorify God in the day of visitation.

So what have you become?

And what are you to do? And why?

Are you beginning to see the practical outworking of it all? It thrills our hearts to share these transforming truths with you, Beloved of God, royal priesthood!

Tomorrow we'll wrap it up as we look at how your practical holiness is "worked out," as Philippians 2:12-13 says.

TAKE AWAY

Think through what you've observed today and talk to God about it. Tell Him you really want to be holy even as He is holy. Ask Him to show you anything in your life that mars His image in you. It will delight Him and bring Him pleasure (2 Corinthians 5:9).

Is Holiness a Process?

KAY

Holiness—sanctification—is a position as well as a process. As we saw, when we receive Jesus Christ, believe and accept Him as our God and Savior, we are then sanctified once and for all.

Yet in another sense, that's only the beginning of the story.

You become "holier than thou" (or what thou once was)! As we saw in Hebrews 10, we are *being* sanctified. It's a process, so don't be discouraged. It's also a battle. With this in mind, Peter reminds us that we are to abstain from fleshly lusts which wage war against the soul (1 Peter 2:11). Don't surrender. Don't wave a white flag to your rebellious flesh. Remember, God has made it possible to win the war. It is won through our union with Christ and living in the light of it.

According to Romans 6:1-11, we were so united with Christ that when He died, we died. Our old self was crucified. When He was buried, we were buried. When He was raised from the dead, we were united in His resurrection. Consequently we are no longer slaves to sin. Ours is but to act on this fact...and to live it out in faith. How do we do this? Listen to Romans 6:19. Mark *sanctification* as you did *holy.*

> For just as you presented your members as slaves to
>
> impurity and to lawlessness, resulting in further law-
>
> lessness, so now present your members as slaves to
>
> righteousness, resulting in sanctification.

We don't have to yield to sin; we can be separate from it—holy. It happens moment by moment, opportunity by opportunity, with a decision to walk in obedience to God in the power of the Spirit. The Spirit dwelling within gives you the power to resist sin.

Dealing with the "Old Man"

Ephesians 4:22-23 tells us that in reference to your former manner of life, you laid aside the old self—the old man, the old you, the one who died with Christ, the one corrupted by the lusts of deceit. So now what do you do? You are to keep on being renewed in the spirit of your mind. What does that mean? It means that you are to fill yourself with the truth of God's Word, hang on to His every word, and live by His precepts. You are to live according to who you are now! The new creation. The new self. The one created in the likeness of God in righteousness and holiness of the truth. You are no longer to live the way the rest of the unsaved world lives; rather you are to live out the truth of what God has done and has given you the power to do: *to be holy as He is holy.*

And what does that look like practically? It looks like obeying Ephesians 4:25–5:2. We looked at some of these verses earlier in our study, but it would be good to stop right now and list below the behaviors God covers in these verses. Just bullet-point them. Say them aloud as you list them. As you do, you'll see they line up as dos and don'ts, but don't mistake this for legalism. It's not. It's the holiness of truth, practical obedience.

Perfecting Holiness

In 2 Corinthians 7:1, Paul writes, "Let us cleanse ourselves from all defilement of flesh and spirit, perfecting holiness in the fear of

God." When it comes to perfecting holiness, there is so much we could look at of a practical nature. Since space is limited in these few pages, however, let's just zero in on a few highlights.

First, watch the company you keep. People can have a great influence on us. Have godly friends. Keep company with people who, like you, are pursing holiness. First Corinthians 15:33 tells us that evil companions corrupt good morals, and 2 Corinthians 6:14-18, which leads right into 2 Corinthians 7:1, warns us about being "bound, yoked together" with unbelievers.

Look at 2 Corinthians 6:14–7:1. As you do, underline everything we are not to do and circle what we are to do.

14 Do not be bound together with unbelievers; for what partnership have righteousness and lawlessness, or what fellowship has light with darkness?

15 Or what harmony has Christ with Belial, or what has a believer in common with an unbeliever?

16 Or what agreement has the temple of God with idols? For we are the temple of the living God; just as God said,

"I WILL DWELL IN THEM AND WALK AMONG THEM; AND I WILL BE THEIR GOD, AND THEY SHALL BE MY PEOPLE.

17 "Therefore, COME OUT FROM THEIR MIDST AND BE SEPARATE," says the Lord.

"AND DO NOT TOUCH WHAT IS UNCLEAN; and I will welcome you.

18 "And I will be a father to you, and you shall be sons and daughters to Me," says the Lord Almighty.

7:1 Therefore, having these promises, beloved, let us cleanse ourselves from all defilement of flesh and spirit, perfecting holiness in the fear of God.

Do you see, Beloved, how we have come full circle, back to clean versus unclean—the separation that holiness brings and befits us as God's children?

Second, keep yourself sexually pure. One of the key areas where perfecting holiness is being violated by those who profess Christ is sexual immorality. Look at 1 Thessalonians 4:3-8 and mark the references to *sanctification*.

3 For this is the will of God, your sanctification; that is, that you abstain from sexual immorality;

4 that each of you know how to possess his own vessel in sanctification and honor,

5 not in lustful passion, like the Gentiles who do not know God;

6 and that no man transgress and defraud his brother in the matter because the Lord is the avenger in all these things, just as we also told you before and solemnly warned you.

7 For God has not called us for the purpose of impurity, but in sanctification.

8 So, he who rejects this is not rejecting man but the
God who gives His Holy Spirit to you.

What do you learn from marking *sanctification*? Sanctification
in what aspect of our lives?

And what are the consequences if you reject this truth and give
in to immorality? Whom do you have to deal with and why?

We will talk about sexual morality in greater depth on Day 21,
so I won't go any further right now. Just know that this is an area of
great weakness in the professing church today, and God does not
want us to be deceived.

Listen to what Paul writes about not being deceived in
1 Corinthians 6:9-11. As you read it mark the word *sanctified*.

9 Or do you not know that the unrighteous will not
inherit the kingdom of God? Do not be deceived;
neither fornicators, nor idolaters, nor adulterers, nor
effeminate, nor homosexuals,

10 nor thieves, nor the covetous, nor drunkards, nor
revilers, nor swindlers, will inherit the kingdom of
God.

11 Such were some of you; but you were washed, but you

were sanctified, but you were justified in the name of
the Lord Jesus Christ and in the Spirit of our God.

Did you notice the list of those who will not inherit the kingdom of God, who will not go to heaven? And did you underline *sanctified*? What do you learn from these verses?

As I said, we'll go into this more on Day 21. I simply want you to see today the critical link between sexuality and sanctification.

Third, you perfect holiness by living under control of the Spirit. Some wonder how anyone can perfect holiness when we live in a body of flesh. The answer is, we are to walk by the Spirit, as Galatians 5:16 says. A careful reading of Galatians 5:22 and examination of the nine-fold fruit of the Spirit shows us that God gives us self-control.

Fourth, holiness is perfected by love. Listen to 1 Thessalonians 3:12-13: "May the Lord cause you to increase and abound in love for one another, and for all people, just as we also do for you; so that He may establish your hearts without blame in holiness before our God and Father at the coming of our Lord Jesus with all His saints."

TAKE AWAY

It's love, Beloved, love for one another that demonstrates His holiness and manifests the reality of God in us. Remember, this is how people know we are His disciples: We have love for one another. As you abound in love, you live out holiness. Remember the fruit of the Spirit is love. So love. Love as Jesus loved. Pick out someone to love on—someone who needs it. Let them experience His love through you.

What Is Spiritual Warfare?

KAY

From the very beginning there's been a battle raging between God and the serpent of old for the heart, the allegiance, of mankind. If you understand the battle, the players, and the battlefield, it will make you only stronger.

So let's go back to the beginning: Genesis, the book of beginnings. Genesis is the foundation stone of the 66 books that make up the Bible. Revelation, the final book, is the capstone. What you see begun in Genesis, you see finalized in Revelation. If you've sat under my teaching, you know I am somehow famous for taking you from Genesis and going to Revelation when I teach. It's become a joke among the Precept students! I am determined we will know the whole counsel of God—and how it fits together. If it was critical to Paul, it is critical to us.

The books of the Bible in the original languages of Hebrew, Aramaic, and Greek are the very words of God—words that according to Jesus came from the mouth of God (Matthew 4:4). They are pure words, uncontaminated by man and preserved by God through the generations.

Yet, as you are undoubtedly aware, that fact has been contested again and again. The father of casting doubts on the veracity of God's Word is Satan himself, and one of his agents was Julius Wellhausen, a German theologian, Old Testament scholar, and the father of higher criticism.

In 1878 a chilling wind of doubt blew across Europe and crossed the Atlantic Ocean, bringing a storm of distrust and spiritual disquiet to America's shores and the minds and hearts of men. Until that time the Bible was a book trusted to be the Word of God. Then the deathly words of the serpent of old, "Has God said?" were heard around the world. Through the theories of higher criticism, the reason of man seemingly superseded the Word of God. Many seminaries became cemeteries as they moved from divine revelation to human reasoning, and as professors diminished the veracity of the Bible. God's words that were spirit and life were deemed subservient to higher criticism, the deliberations of finite man!

It was a return to the taunting question from the serpent of old. Although the serpent's words are recorded in Genesis 3, you need to read them in the context of the preceding chapters. As you read, it will help to mark the following key words. You can underline or circle them or you can use the following suggestions:

Mark every reference to

- *God* with a triangle △ (or color yellow)
- *man* like this ♂ (or color orange)
- *woman* like this ♀ (or color pink)
- *the serpent* like this 𝒲 (in red)
- *die* with a tombstone like this ⌓

When you mark a word, also mark any pronouns or synonyms in the same manner.

Genesis 1:27

> God created man in His own image, in the image of
> God He created him; male and female He created
> them.

Genesis 2:15-17

15 Then the LORD God took the man and put him into the garden of Eden to cultivate it and keep it.

16 The LORD God commanded the man, saying, "From any tree of the garden you may eat freely;

17 but from the tree of the knowledge of good and evil you shall not eat, for in the day that you eat from it you will surely die."

Genesis 3:1-13

1 Now the serpent was more crafty than any beast of the field which the LORD God had made. And he said to the woman, "Indeed, has God said, 'You shall not eat from any tree of the garden'?"

2 The woman said to the serpent, "From the fruit of the trees of the garden we may eat;

3 but from the fruit of the tree which is in the middle of the garden, God has said, 'You shall not eat from it or touch it, or you will die.'"

4 The serpent said to the woman, "You surely will not die!

5 "For God knows that in the day you eat from it your eyes will be opened, and you will be like God, knowing good and evil."

6 When the woman saw that the tree was good for food, and that it was a delight to the eyes, and that the tree was desirable to make one wise, she took from its fruit and ate; and she gave also to her husband with her, and he ate.

7 Then the eyes of both of them were opened, and they knew that they were naked; and they sewed fig leaves together and made themselves loin coverings.

8 They heard the sound of the Lord God walking in the garden in the cool of the day, and the man and his wife hid themselves from the presence of the Lord God among the trees of the garden.

9 Then the Lord God called to the man, and said to him, "Where are you?"

10 He said, "I heard the sound of You in the garden, and I was afraid because I was naked; so I hid myself."

11 And He said, "Who told you that you were naked? Have you eaten from the tree of which I commanded you not to eat?"

12 The man said, "The woman whom You gave to be with me, she gave me from the tree, and I ate."

13 Then the Lord God said to the woman, "What is this you have done?" And the woman said, "The serpent deceived me, and I ate."

Now what do you learn from marking the following?

Man	Woman	The Serpent

The Bible is a progressive revelation—truth in all its beauty and majesty unfolds throughout each of its books. Thus Scripture becomes the best interpreter of Scripture. And since the Word of God is absolute truth, you'll see that, when studied in context, Scripture never contradicts Scripture. It brings wonder and often tears to my eyes as I read it. I am so very awed at God and so thankful that He chose me for Himself and wants me to know truth.

Having let you get a glimpse at my heart, let's look at other Scriptures that give us greater insight into the serpent who deceived Eve.

By the way, when Adam listened to Eve and ate the forbidden fruit, Romans 5:12 tells us that sin entered into the world. Adam and Eve became sinners—it was in their genes, so to speak. Therefore, when they reproduced, they produced sinners. And what did this bring? Death. The sin of Adam and Eve resulted in death for all mankind.

It all came because Eve believed a lie.

WHAT DOES GOD TELL US IN HIS WORD ABOUT THE SERPENT?

As you read the following verses, mark every reference to *the serpent,* including pronouns and synonyms (*dragon, devil, Satan, god of this world*), with a red pitchfork as you did before.

Revelation nails the identity of the serpent, so let's begin with the end, the last book of the Bible.

Revelation 12:7-10

> 7 And there was war in heaven, Michael and his angels waging war with the dragon. The dragon and his angels waged war,
>
> 8 and they were not strong enough, and there was no longer a place found for them in heaven.
>
> 9 And the great dragon was thrown down, the serpent of old who is called the devil and Satan, who deceives the whole world; he was thrown down to the earth, and his angels were thrown down with him.
>
> 10 Then I heard a loud voice in heaven, saying,
>
> "Now the salvation, and the power, and the kingdom of our God and the authority of His Christ have come, for the accuser of our brethren has been thrown down, he who accuses them before our God day and night."

Now go to the end of this day, recording what you learn about the serpent of old under the heading "Insights on the Serpent" on page 154. Do this as you finish observing each Scripture.

John 8:43-47 (Jesus is speaking here to Jews who were seeking to kill Him.) Mark every reference to the *devil* (and synonyms) with a red pitchfork.

43 "Why do you not understand what I am saying? It is because you cannot hear My word.

44 "You are of your father the devil, and you want to do the desires of your father. He was a murderer from the beginning, and does not stand in the truth because there is no truth in him. Whenever he speaks a lie, he speaks from his own nature, for he is a liar and the father of lies.

45 "But because I speak the truth, you do not believe Me.

46 "Which one of you convicts Me of sin? If I speak truth, why do you not believe Me?

47 "He who is of God hears the words of God; for this reason you do not hear them, because you are not of God."

2 Corinthians 4:3-4

3 And even if our gospel is veiled, it is veiled to those who are perishing,

4 in whose case the god of this world has blinded the minds of the unbelieving so that they might not see the light of the gospel of the glory of Christ, who is the image of God.

Ephesians 2:1-2

1 And you were dead in your trespasses and sins,

2 in which you formerly walked according to the course of this world, according to the prince of the power of the air, of the spirit that is now working in the sons of disobedience.

1 John 5:19

19 We know that we are of God, and that the whole world lies in the power of the evil one.

Yes, the whole world lies in Satan's power. The people of this world are by nature children of wrath, puppets on Satan's string. But not us! Not anymore. Once we believe, truly believe from the core of our being, we are rescued from the domain of darkness and transferred into the kingdom of God's beloved Son.

Our sins are forgiven—paid for once and for all! Paid for by Jesus' death and verified by His resurrection. Therefore, when you receive Jesus Christ as the Son of God, your Savior, according to Hebrews 2:14-15, the devil's power over you is broken. You belong to God's forever family. Christ is in you, the hope of glory. This mortal will put on immortality, and you will live forever and ever. But know this: In the meantime, in between time, you've got a war on your hands!

My second son, Mark, and I love to watch war movies. There's much to learn that transfers to our spiritual life. One imperative is to know your enemy. You see this played out in movies such as *Patton, The Desert Fox, Midway,* and *A Bridge Too Far.* It's called military intelligence.

Many people wrongly imagine that if they don't know anything about the devil or don't study spiritual warfare, the devil won't bother them. Not true! Warfare goes with Christianity, and don't let anyone tell you otherwise. God tells us not to be ignorant of the devil's schemes or tactics.

While it's not in Satan's power to change your eternal destination of heaven, he still wants to wrestle you to the ground and pin you there. The devil doesn't want you on your feet; he wants you facedown in the dirt. As Ephesians 6:12 tells us, "Our struggle is not against flesh and blood, but against the rulers, against the powers, against the world forces of this darkness, against the spiritual forces of wickedness in the heavenly places." The Greek word for "struggle" is *palē*, a wrestling term that means to throw you to the ground and hold you there.

Ephesians 6:10-17 is the classic passage on warfare for the child of God, and yet there is far more to it than just Ephesians 6:10-17.[4] Since *Lord, I Need Answers* is only a 28-day journey, we can't cover this topic thoroughly. David and I realize, however, that if you are going to be spiritually strong, you have to understand that you are at war—so you won't be shocked by the conflict or thrown by the enemy's tactics. In fact, our battles will only intensify as we come closer to the final years that lead to the Day of the Lord.

The devil's main target is your mind—a lesson I learned firsthand soon after I became God's child. I'll share it with you tomorrow, because this is a truth that can't wait. It will help you "stand firm" as Paul says three times, one after another, in Ephesians 6:11,13,14.

So, Beloved, be strong in the Lord and in the strength of His might, put on the full armor of God and you will be "able to stand firm against the schemes of the devil (Ephesians 6:11).

Take Away

It's important to know the basics about your enemy. With the facts in mind, you can spot his activity. List the insights you gained from the Scriptures studied on the devil.

Insights on the Serpent

How Is My Mind Like a Battleground?

KAY

I was just a week or so old in the Lord when Satan's first attack came. I was at my desk at the famous Johns Hopkins Hospital when all of a sudden the thought came to mind, *This is just a bunch of bull.*

I was horrified. The wording, I know, is crude, but I want you to know exactly what hit my mind. Later that evening, tears spilled from my eyes as I told Dave Pantzer what had happened. I felt so unclean, so ashamed to have a thought like that about my newfound faith.

Dave was the first man I knew who was a "walking Bible." He discipled me at the beginning—and of course, I thought I ought to marry him. (But that's another story for another time.)

I'll never forget his laugh and his words, "Oh, Kay, that's *the devil!*" Suddenly, the enemy was exposed. Those weren't my thoughts; they were *his* posing as mine!

Beloved, if you want to stand strong, if you want to stand firm and hold your position as a child of God, you must understand the battle for your mind. Remember what God just taught you from His Word about the serpent of old, the devil, Satan? He is a liar, the father of lies, a murderer, a deceiver, an accuser, the tempter who does not abide in the truth. He will play with truth as he did when he tempted Jesus in the wilderness, but there is always a twist with it, a distortion.

Satan knows you. Remember, you lived under his domain until

you were saved. He was the spirit that worked within you, messing with the desires of your mind. This is what Ephesians 2 teaches.

He knows your weaknesses—where you are vulnerable. He knows how and when to bring your past before you. How well I know that!

One great battle occurred when I was five or six years old in the Lord. I had served on the mission field with my husband, but we had to come home because of a problem with my heart. The Lord in His grace and kindness, however, had supplied us with a 32-acre piece of property, where I had been teaching the Scriptures to teens and adults. It was a joyous time in my life, as we were beginning to see the Lord work in powerful ways.

I can even remember where I was when the enemy's salvo hit me. I was driving across Chickamauga Dam when suddenly, seemingly out of the blue, my past reared its ugly head. In that moment my mind was flooded with details of some of my immoral liaisons. Just that quickly, my joy was obliterated by a cloud of heaviness, a chill of darkness, of contamination. It was a battle for my mind.

I could tell you story after story—a problem with immoral dreams, thoughts twice of suicide, feeling like such a horrible failure, feeling that someone I ministered with on various platforms didn't like me (only to find out years later she felt the same), battling desires, attractions, vanity, worthlessness...on and on. Can you relate? Have you been there, thought that, felt that? Welcome to the family! It's called warfare, and it is the "fare" of every child of God.

Yet let me assure you, there is victory. You and I have all we need to prevail in this warfare. The first thing God taught me was that I have the mind of Christ. The mind of Christ is the ability to know and discern truth, and through the Spirit the power to live in it. Let's look together at this mighty truth. More than anything else, I want you to see it for yourself...and take it into your very life.

Read 1 Corinthians 2:12-16, which is printed below. As you read these liberating words, mark three things:

- Every reference to *we* including any synonyms. The context shows the *we* to be believers in Jesus Christ; so also mark synonyms in the same way (e.g., *he who is spiritual* in verse 15). Mark *we* with a circle or color it orange.
- *The Spirit* when it refers to the Holy Spirit. You can use a symbol like this ⌇⌇⌇ . Color it yellow.
- *Mind* with a lumpy circle like the brain. Something like this: ⬭

1 Corinthians 2:12-16

12 Now we have received, not the spirit of the world, but the Spirit who is from God, so that we may know the things freely given to us by God,

13 which things we also speak, not in words taught by human wisdom, but in those taught by the Spirit, combining spiritual thoughts with spiritual words.

14 But a natural man does not accept the things of the Spirit of God, for they are foolishness to him; and he cannot understand them, because they are spiritually appraised.

15 But he who is spiritual appraises all things, yet he himself is appraised by no one.

16 For who has known the mind of the Lord, that he will instruct Him? But we have the mind of Christ.

Now read the text again. Go ahead and read it out loud; believe it or not, this will really help you to comprehend what you read—and remember more of it. Underline *know* and put a checkmark over every use of *appraise*. To appraise something is to check it out, analyze its worth, its value, its significance.

What two kinds of people are contrasted in this passage? How are they described and why do you think they are described this way?

What do you learn from the text about "the natural man"?

What do you learn from marking *we*—the one who is spiritual, having the Spirit of God within him or her?

Now list below what you learn from marking the references to the *Spirit* and to the *mind*.

Some of the most serious injuries a person can receive are those that affect the brain. Even as I write these words, today's news is running a story about a movie star who has just been declared brain dead after a fall. She had been with her skiing instructor, getting lessons on the bunny slope. She didn't have her helmet on. They wanted her to see a doctor, but she said she was all right—it was no big deal.

But it *was* a big deal. In fact, it was her very life. And if she'd worn a helmet, she would never have been injured at all. It's the same with us in our spiritual battles. In the Ephesians 6 warfare passage I mentioned yesterday, one of the pieces of armor mentioned is "the helmet of salvation." God gives us the mind of Christ so we can appraise—or weigh the worth and value of—all things. And that is what we need to do with our thoughts. Not every thought is from Christ!

Listen to what Paul says as he deals with the Corinthians, some of whom are attacking him with lies and accusations, demeaning his appearance, his speech, his character, his ministry. Read 2 Corinthians 10:3-5 aloud.

3 For though we walk in the flesh, we do not war according to the flesh,

4 for the weapons of our warfare are not of the flesh, but divinely powerful for the destruction of fortresses.

5 We are destroying speculations and every lofty thing raised up against the knowledge of God, and we are taking every thought captive to the obedience of Christ.

Paul declares that he is taking "every thought captive to the obedience of Christ." What does that mean? It means Paul checks out what he is thinking to make sure it's in accord with what God says in His Word about *everything*, including his own position and standing in Christ.

A strong Christian does not entertain every thought that comes to his or her mind. Some of it is trash—out-and-out lies, demoralizing, immobilizing thoughts, immoral or inordinate desires, sensual cravings, disparaging thoughts of worthlessness and condemnation.

Rather, the one who is strong does as Proverbs, the book of wisdom, tells us: He continually guards his heart for out of it are the issues of life (4:23 NKJV).

What a strange battle this is! When you think about normal warfare in the world, you might think about a soldier who engages in a violent firefight and then retreats back to the safety of a reinforced bunker. And there, in that safe place, he is able to relax and be alone with his thoughts. In the physical world, that's a picture of peace and safety. But for the Christian, that's where the battle begins! There is no safety "with our own thoughts," unless we carefully and deliberately filter and evaluate those thoughts with the aid of God's Word and God's Spirit.

In Hebrew thought, the terms "heart" and "mind" are interchangeable. As Proverbs 23:4 says of man, "As he thinks within himself, so he is." Our mind/heart can be a dictator, a despot. That is why it must be carefully guarded. Every thought must be dropped alongside the plumb line of God's Word. Does it line up with truth? *Truth*...not feelings!

Why should we be so careful to check it out? Because of what Jesus teaches us in Matthew 15:18-20. As you read, mark the references to *the heart* and remember, *heart* is a synonym for the mind in this passage.

> 18 "But the things that proceed out of the mouth come from the heart, and those defile the man.
>
> 19 "For out of the heart come evil thoughts, murders, adulteries, fornications, thefts, false witness, slanders.
>
> 20 "These are the things which defile the man..."

Using a stick figure, draw what this passage is teaching.

What kind of imaginations, fears, or disturbing, tormenting thoughts are you dealing with? Write them out, and then we will deal with them in a few minutes.

As you saw in 1 Corinthians 2, we have the mind of Christ, but we have to protect its borders. We can't let imaginations and thoughts contrary to truth invade our mind. If they do, we'll experience torment rather than the peace that God intends for us. They will gang up on us, try to destroy us, and rob us of our joy. They'll seek to enslave us and make us their servants. And in doing so, they will keep us from serving Christ as we should. (One quick illustration is pornography. Surely you have heard the horror stories—or maybe, because of disobedience, you've experienced them. I pray not, but if so, then this will help you.)

A passage that has helped me greatly in winning the battle for the mind is the fourth and final chapter of Paul's letter to the Philippians. Read it aloud, watching the flow of thought. Underline every instruction you see. As you do, remember anxiety is a matter of the mind that can raise havoc in the body.

4 Rejoice in the Lord always; again I will say, rejoice!

5 Let your gentle spirit be known to all men. The Lord is near.

6 Be anxious for nothing, but in everything by prayer and supplication with thanksgiving let your requests be made known to God.

7 And the peace of God, which surpasses all comprehension, will guard your hearts and your minds in Christ Jesus.

8 Finally, brethren, whatever is true, whatever is honorable, whatever is right, whatever is pure, whatever is
lovely, whatever is of good repute, if there is any excellence and if anything worthy of praise, dwell on these
things [literally "ponder these things"].

9 The things you have learned and received and heard
and seen in me, practice these things, and the God of
peace will be with you.

When our minds are troubled, we find ourselves experiencing
stress, anxiety, sleeplessness…and a short temper. Yet this is not the
way God wants us to live. We are to rejoice. God is not far off; He is
near and He is God. You are not to fear, be anxious, worry—not for
even one thing! As Philippians 4:6 says, "Be anxious for nothing,"
which in the Greek reads "Stop being anxious."

But how do you do this when your mind is like a racehorse in
the starting gate, champing at the bit, snorting and carrying on?
Paul tells you.

First, pray. The Greek word for prayer is *proseuchē,* which is a
reference to general prayer. Stop and talk to God about who He
is and what He has promised. You see Jehoshaphat doing that in
2 Chronicles 20 when a huge army is coming against him. And God
shows up as God!

Second, be very specific in your petition. Supplication is *deēsis*—
tell God what exactly you are dealing with, what is tormenting you,
what you need. Nail it by naming it. "Let your requests be known
to God."

Third, thank Him. Thanksgiving shows that you believe God,
that you trust Him, that you know He will show up as God. Thanksgiving is faith in action.

I remember a time when David was a boy and we thought we'd

lost him. He didn't show up for dinner one evening. As we've mentioned, Precept Ministries International (then called Reach Out) is on 32 acres with a creek, some woods, and all sorts of places for boys to enjoy God's wonderful outdoors. His father was rather casual about David's not showing up, but I became anxious. This wasn't typical David, mischievous as he may have been! We had called and called, but he hadn't come.

A terrible storm was approaching, and I couldn't wait any longer. We hopped in the car just before the rain started pelting us. The sky was ominous, getting blacker by the minute as the wind furiously whipped the trees. I didn't know where my son was. I soon took on the character of the storm—dark, furious, blowing like the wind—because Jack hadn't become concerned sooner.

We combed the neighborhoods, the window rolled down, screaming his name into the wind, while my mind went crazy. A young boy had just been killed in Chattanooga, his body found in a wooded area behind his house. Was the killer in our neighborhood?

Then Philippians 4 came to mind, and I came to my senses. I called on everything I knew about God, especially His sovereignty and His omnipotence. From there I began asking Him to protect David, to remind David of what we had taught him about God, about His power, about calling out to Him for protection, about God's sovereignty. I asked God to keep him calm, to remind him to pray, and to help him deal with anyone who was threatening him. Finally, when I had emptied myself of my petitions, supplications, requests, I began to thank God—to thank Him for the promise that it would all work together for good, even if it wasn't good, and that it would be used to make me more like Christ. I stopped being mad at Jack and asked his forgiveness.

As we drove and continued to look, I "Philippians 4:8-ed" it—just as I had taught others to do. To "Philippians 4:8" something is the *fourth* thing you do when your mind is troubled. I frisked—did a pat down—on the thoughts at the door of my mind to make sure they met the criteria of Philippians 4:8. And if they didn't, I wouldn't allow them in. I wouldn't entertain them. I would not dwell on, ponder, or think about them. Were they true? Maybe so, but were they also honorable, right, pure, lovely, of good repute? Were they excellent? Anything worthy of praise?

If one single thing was missing, it wasn't allowed in my mind.

As you know, we found our David. He had been taking care of his playmate in the storm, trying to lead him back home.

It was and is a battle as the devil bangs away at the door of your mind, yelling, screaming, threatening, cajoling, enticing, telling you that you can't survive without _____ (whatever), that you'll die if you don't _____, that you have to have it, and telling you God doesn't love you, doesn't care. Hissing, "God's holding out on you."

But don't give in to the liar, the deceiver, the murderer. *Resist him.* Stand firm with the door bolted. What that serpent has with him is a pile of bricks to build a stronghold in your mind—a fortress of thoughts, destructive imaginations from which he can besiege you from within and take you captive.

Remember, my friend, *the battle is already won.* The Captain of the Hosts, Jehovah Shabuoth, is on your side, and He has won the battle. Stand firm in His full armor.

When I teach people about the battle for the mind and show them how to "Philippians 4:8" it, I often refer to the radio dramas from my childhood. In those days, radio was the nightly entertainment hub of almost every American family. We didn't even get a television set until I was 12. But how I loved those radio dramas: *Gangbusters, Inner Sanctum* (with its chilling squeaky door), *Fibber McGee and Molly,* and *Jack Armstrong, the All American Boy.* Another program (I think it was called *Beulah*) always included a character named Bill knocking at the door. You would hear the knock, and then this coy feminine voice would call out, "Who's that knockin' at my door?" The reply was always the same, "It's Bill, baby; no pain, no strain!"

It's nice to be hospitable and open the door when someone knocks, but when it comes to certain thoughts knocking on the door of your mind, don't open that door until you know who or what is knocking! Don't automatically offer southern hospitality and say, "Come on in. Sit down and have some tea." Always ask, "Who's that knockin' at my door?" Because if it's the devil, he's got a load of bricks with him—thoughts contrary to truth—and he's out to build a stronghold in your mind.

I remember one day when Jack greatly disappointed me. I had cleaned his office, decorated it, and given him a clean sheet on his desk pad that said in beautiful big handwriting, "Surprise, love you, darling."

You know how it is when you imagine someone's response? I had pictured him being so delighted he would take me in his arms and tell me how wonderful, thoughtful, and caring I was, and how blessed he was to have me as his wife.

It's a nice picture, but that's not what happened. In fact, Jack wasn't thrilled at all with what I'd done. Instead, he questioned me—what had I done with his desk pad, and this and that, and on and on. Stunned by this response, I replied that I wasn't stupid and that it was all there in the drawer of his desk.

With that, he walked into the bathroom to brush his teeth and get ready for bed. No thanks. No adoring. No conversation. Not so much as a smile.

He had left me alone, with no one to talk to…but then again, I did have someone to talk to. The devil was pounding on the door, and I let him in.

"He doesn't understand you, does he?"

"No!"

"You probably shouldn't have married him, should you?"

"Nope."

"And furthermore—"

And I said, "Hand me another brick!"

I was about to build a fortress—a stronghold of "let's trash Jack."

Remember the verse in Ephesians 4:26-27? "Be angry and yet do not sin; do not let the sun go down on your anger, and do not give the devil an opportunity." I had a real battle on my hands that night. Would I continue to give opportunity to the devil, allowing him to create a stronghold in my thoughts against my own husband? Would I disobey Scripture by allowing the anger to simmer overnight—perhaps turning into bitterness by morning?

Later, I crawled into bed after I was sure Jack was asleep. I had opened the door to the devil and listened to his voice. How was I to now eject him from my thoughts? In fact, I couldn't do it—not alone! The next morning, I had to invite Jesus into my thoughts, to shield my mind, and to change my heart. And He did!

Take Away

All of us have walked through those metal detectors at the airport—it's a common part of travel in these safety-conscious days. In the same way, we need to send our thoughts through the detector of God's powerful Word. Don't let a single one "on board" until you've checked it through security! Keep your mind on red alert against the terrorist attacks of the evil one and his army of demons. Think about how the devil comes at you. What thoughts does he try to get you to dwell on? What makes you miserable? What brings you down?

The next time those thoughts line up outside your mind, asking for admittance, make them pass through the "thought detector" of Philippians 4:8. If they don't pass the tests of that passage, turn them away!

Trials: How Am I Supposed to Get Through Them?

KAY

My first really hard trial as a new Christian came when I picked up the phone on a Sunday afternoon and heard my father-in-law say, "Tom is dead. He hanged himself."

As I told you earlier, God had brought me to the place as a new Christian where I had been willing to go back to my husband. I would discover later that Tom had bipolar disorder. (We called it "manic depression" in those days.) I worked at the Toledo State Hospital for my psychiatric training while I was dating Tom, caring for and treating many who were manic-depressive. But Tom certainly didn't act like those deeply troubled people at all. I don't think it became an issue in his life until just before we got married.

Tom had had an episode of anger that seemed so unlike him it made me wonder what I was getting myself into. But I quickly dismissed it. I couldn't admit that I had made a wrong choice. Oh, the stranglehold of pride!

With the news of Tom's suicide also came the memory of the two times he had threatened suicide over the phone, to which I had replied, "Do a good job so I get your money." I wasn't a Christian when I said it, yet it wasn't said so that he would actually kill himself. Rather, this was the psychology of the day—*bluff them out of it, make them mad, and they won't kill themselves.*

Not only did I have to deal with what I had said to Tom, but I also had to deal with a heart that was ready to return to my husband, to start again with a truly fine and talented man, to rebuild my family. God had graciously brought me to my knees in submission to His will, so my one consolation in Tom's suicide was that I had been willing to go back if that was what God wanted. What hurt me the most was the realization that I had intended to write to Tom, to tell him that I was willing to come back. But...I hadn't gotten around to it.

Can you understand, Beloved, what was going on—the battle in my mind, the test of my faith?

I hung up the phone and tried to call my pastor. He wasn't there. I slid to my knees beside the bed and cried out to God. I don't remember what I said, but I do remember what *God* said. And I'm so grateful He spoke clearly!

Three verses I had read came to my mind. I didn't know where they were in the Bible, but God brought to mind what I had read in His Word. The first was a Scripture I had memorized, 1 Corinthians 10:13:

> No temptation has overtaken you but such as is common to man; and God is faithful, who will not allow you to be tempted beyond what you are able, but with the temptation will provide the way of escape also, so that you will be able to endure it.

TRIALS COME WITH BEING A CHRISTIAN

Trials, testings, and temptations are part of the package with salvation in Christ. You can't escape them, and when you understand their purpose, you realize you really don't want to escape them, no matter how difficult they may be. Their purpose is not to destroy you but to make you like Jesus. To make you spiritually strong.

Let's stop and look at trials and testings, and then I'll continue with my story.

First, the word for temptation in 1 Corinthians 10:13 is *peirasmos*. It's defined as "a trial, temptation, putting to the test, a trial of one's character." *Peirasmos* is used in James 1:2 where it is translated "trials." Read James 1:2-4 and see for yourself what God tells you to do and why. Underline *my brethren, you,* and *your.*

2 Consider it all joy, my brethren, when you encounter various trials,

3 knowing that the testing of your faith produces endurance.

4 And let endurance have its perfect result, so that you may be perfect and complete, lacking in nothing.

Write down your observations.

Who is being addressed in these verses?

What are they to do?

Why are they to do it?

The word translated "endurance" is *hupomenō*—it means "to abide (*meno*) under (*hupo*)." From it came my exhortation in many Precept courses, "Hangeth thou in there." (Sometimes it was, "Hangeth thou in there, O baby!") Got the picture? It's a young kitten with a look of fright hanging by its claws from a limb.

ENDURANCE IN A TRIAL

Endurance is steadfastness. It means you don't quit, give up, or cease to be what you should be. Steadfast endurance is what God uses to make you strong, complete, not lacking in anything. It grows you up, matures you. So how are you to handle and respond to trials? You are to count it all joy. I know it sounds like idiocy, and it *would* be if you didn't look at these challenging, hard, and often painful situations from God's perspective.

First Peter 1:6-7 tells us much the same. In Peter's passage, however, there's an added tidbit you don't want to miss. As you read it aloud, underline every *you* and *your*.

> 6 In this you greatly rejoice, even though now for a little
>
> while, if necessary, you have been distressed by vari-
>
> ous trials,
>
> 7 so that the proof of your faith, being more precious
>
> than gold which is perishable, even though tested by
>
> fire, may be found to result in praise and glory and
>
> honor at the revelation of Jesus Christ;

Now, my friend, what did you learn from marking the *you* and the *your*? List your finds below. The very doing of it helps seal its truth in your mind.

Did you see "for a little while"? What does this tell us? Please hear this, Beloved: *Every trial has a beginning AND an end.* To gain the full benefit from the trial—all that God in His grace and goodness intends for you—endure! It will have an end.

Did you see "if necessary"? What does that tell you? God thinks that particular trial is necessary for you to be all you should be or to be more effective in your service and ministry to others. You can rest assured, then, that no trial, no matter what it is, is without purpose. It's been filtered through God's sovereign fingers of love, and it is the very thing you need in order to become what He wants you to become.

REAL FAITH IS PROVEN

Did you notice the phrase "the proof of your faith"? Why do we need to *prove* faith? Because faith isn't even seen to be faith until it is tested. We can say that we love God and that we want to serve Him and be used of Him, we can tell others of His grace and sufficiency and promises, and we can say that His Word is true and to be trusted. That telling, of course, is good. Encouraging others in their trials is good.

But what happens when *we're* the ones in the fire? What happens when the roof caves in on *our* world? Will our faith prove genuine? Will we pass the test? "Hanging thou in there" shows the reality of your faith.

You need to also remember that God intends for you to pass the test. When I teach a required course on Bible study methods at Tennessee Temple University, you can rest assured I want all my students to ace the course. The exams, however, aren't easy. How my students do in their exams lets me know how they're progressing—if they're really getting a grasp on the course content. But the test results also show me what kind of a teacher I am.

God wants you to ace His tests. He's a teacher, a coach who wants you to take home the gold. Your trials are *not* more than you can bear. We have His word on that! You can pass every test, and when you do, you are stronger for it.

And what does it bring? Praise, honor, and glory to Him and to you. Graduation! And the honors come when you see Him face-to-face.

Romans 5:2-5, which covers the same truths, gives us another insight on tribulations as it tells us we are to exult in them. "Tribulation brings about perseverance [there it is again]; and perseverance, proven character." In other words, you are put to the test and approved—you pass, you're genuine. Don't you love it when people tell others you are "the real thing," that what they see is what they get? What an affirming thing to hear. No, it doesn't mean you are perfect by any means, but it means you are genuine. And there's a lot to be said for that.

And what comes from proven character? Listen, as Paul is not finished yet: "...and proven character, hope; and hope does not disappoint, because the love of God has been poured out within our hearts through the Holy Spirit who was given to us." Persevering through trials, tribulations, testings, and temptations gives hope. Hope because it demonstrates that the love of God is in your heart and the Holy Spirit is in residence. Remember, the Spirit is the guarantee that you are headed for heaven, for glory (Ephesians 1:13-14).

Right after this call to exult in the hope of the glory of God and in tribulations, God reminds us of what we were before He found us and saved us: helpless and ungodly (Romans 5:6), sinners (5:8), enemies (5:10). And now look at us! Justified by faith (5:1), standing permanently in the grace of God (5:2), and exulting in hope (5:2).

Now, is that enough to help you stand strong? God has you covered! No wonder Paul wanted to experience the fellowship of Jesus' sufferings (Philippians 3:7-11). No wonder, after Paul reminded Timothy of his faith, love, perseverance, persecutions, and sufferings, among other things (2 Timothy 3:10-11), God had Paul tell Timothy that "all who desire to live godly in Christ Jesus will be persecuted" (3:12).

TRANSFERABLE COURAGE?

Paul's life gave courage to Timothy even as yours will to others. And how we need to see living examples of Christians who are strong and courageous. Jesus did the same with the eleven before He was arrested and crucified. He taught them very special truths they needed to remember and cling to, and then He brought it to a close saying, "These things I have spoken to you, so that in Me you may have peace. In the world you have tribulation, but take courage; I have overcome the world" (John 16:33).

Are you going through a trial? Being tested? Enduring tribulation? Have you counted it all joy? Have you rejoiced? Exulted? If not, when we finish today, you may want to get on your knees and do just that.

Let's go back now to that first major trial I described, Tom's suicide. When I heard the news about Tom and fell to my knees, the *second* Scripture that came to my mind was "In everything give thanks, for this is the will of God in Christ Jesus concerning you." I didn't know it was 1 Thessalonians 5:18, but I knew it was God. Remember, Dave Pantzer (the man who discipled me) had told me God held me in His hand and nothing could touch me without His permission. My response of faith was, "God, I don't understand, but I thank You."

I would say that again when I lost a job for sharing my faith. The director of nurses didn't want to let me go; she just wanted me to shut up about Jesus. But I couldn't. And what happened? I got a much better job with long weekends instead of working every night, all night.

I said it when they closed a diagnostic hospital for a weekend and I needed the money. That's the night when, because I wasn't working, I saw Jack Arthur for the first time, the man God had told me five or six months earlier I was going to marry. Until then, all I had was a picture on his missionary prayer card.

It's what I said when we were missionaries in Mexico and someone stole the tires off our new truck in broad daylight. I don't ever remember seeing any particular benefit out of that distressing incident. However...I do recall remaining faithful to trust and thank the Lord in the middle of that trial, which helped my husband. Whether we see the benefit or not, God sees, and we really have an audience of only One to please, don't we? How I love Isaiah 45:6-7:

> "There is no one besides Me;
> I am the Lord, and there is no other.
> The One forming light and creating darkness,

Causing well-being and creating calamity,
I am the LORD who does all these."

If God does these things, I can give thanks in everything.

I can rest because I know who God is—He's not a God who is far off; He is a God who is near. I'd rather have Him in charge than fate, Satan, or Mother Nature, wouldn't you?

A SONG WORTH SINGING—EVEN IN A TRIAL

The song of Moses, found in Deuteronomy 32, is also a blessed reminder of why I can give thanks even in the hardest of situations. When Moses was instructed to write this song, he knew God was going to take him home. Because Moses had not treated God as holy and had struck the rock when he was supposed to speak to it, God told Moses he could not take the children of Israel into the Promised Land. He was 120 years old. The last 80 years of his life led him toward the Promised Land, and although he begged God to let him enter, God said no. Moses would look at Canaan from a distance and die on Mount Nebo, and Joshua, his disciple, would take the nation of Israel over the Jordan into the land.

Yet Moses sang his song! Listen to just a small portion of it, and once again you'll see why we can give thanks in everything:

> "See now that I, I am He,
> And there is no god besides Me;
> It is I who put to death and give life.
> I have wounded and it is I who heal,
> And there is no one who can deliver from
> My hand" (Deuteronomy 32:39).

God has life and death in His hands—wounds and healings—and we, like Israel, are inscribed on the palms of His hands in covenant love (Isaiah 49:16). Of course we can give thanks in everything, for it is the will of God in Christ Jesus concerning me...concerning you. Giving thanks is faith in its highest form, especially when it's hard and seemingly incredible to do so. In the book of Hebrews, God tells us how: "Through Him then, let us continually offer up a sacrifice of praise to God, that is the fruit of lips that give thanks to His name" (Hebrews 13:15).

It is truly a sacrifice, but one that is reasonable when you understand the third thing God spoke to my heart when my 31-year-old husband hanged himself on a closet door.

TRIALS ARE GOOD FOR ME?

How do you live with something like that? You live by every word that comes out of the mouth of God. The third and last verse God gave to me that terrible afternoon was a phrase from Romans 8:28, that "all things work together for good." I didn't know the whole passage, but I found it later in the day and came to a more complete understanding of what God was saying to me. Let's read it together.

> And we know that God causes all things to work
> together for good to those who love God, to those who
> are called according to His purpose.

I hope you noticed that God did *not* say, "All things are good." Of course they're not.

Some things are evil, desperately wicked, from the muck of the pit of hell. Yet a Sovereign God, One who is holy and wise beyond the finite limits of our human understanding, tells us that *all* things keep on working together (the tense of "causes" is present, continuous action) for good.

In His sovereign omniscience and omnipotence, God is able to do this. And what are the "all things"? I believe it dates back to our beginning—to the sperm and the egg that made us "us"—right on through death. Remember what we learned from Ephesians 1? God chose us in Christ before the foundation of the world. His unseen hand has been on us from the beginning, even bringing us to salvation when it pleased Him.

I also believe the "all things" includes even our mistakes, our foibles. Yes, people have the power of choice and are certainly responsible and accountable for what they do. We do have free will. How does this mesh with the sovereignty of God? Quite honestly, you and I may not be able to reconcile those two concepts—both biblical—in this life. But here is something to consider very carefully: If we would be wise and strong, we will embrace the sovereignty of God in faith, even when we can't explain it or rationalize it. We must continue to believe and embrace the whole counsel of God. When we do, faith is able to trust God when He says all things will work together for good.

And just what is that good? That's where God takes us next in the verses that follow: Romans 8:29-30. Read them carefully, you who love God and are called according to His purpose.

> 29 For those whom He foreknew, He also predestined to become conformed to the image of His Son, so that He would be the firstborn among many brethren;
>
> 30 and these whom He predestined, He also called; and these whom He called, He also justified; and these whom He justified, He also glorified.

Isn't God gracious to let us have this insight? Doesn't it cause your heart to swell in gratitude that He would allow us to see the big picture of our lives? To understand that He foreknew us—knew us beforehand—and that He would so carefully weave everything in such a way and mark it out beforehand in His omniscience? And then that He would use it all—the good, the bad, the ugly, the traumatic, even the stupid—to make us more like Jesus? That He would make us what the Holy Trinity—Father, Son, and Holy Spirit—had in mind when He made man in His image, according to His likeness, as Genesis 1:26 says?

It awes me. It puts me on my face before Him.

God predestined me, called me, justified me (declared a sinner righteous because of faith in His Son and His sacrifice), and glorifies me. I am fitted for heaven! Now, this is true for you, Beloved, if you are His child. So go back and read the previous sentence aloud, and then talk to God about it. As you do, remember what else God says through the apostle Paul in Romans 8:31-32:

> 31 What then shall we say to these things? If God is for us, who is against us?
>
> 32 He who did not spare His own Son, but delivered Him over for us all, how will He not also with Him freely give us all things?

You can rest assured that if God gave the ultimate of gifts, His own Son, then He'll give you everything you need. Now that ought to make you strong—no matter what comes your way!

TAKE AWAY

Why don't you get on your knees and thank God for your trials and His promises that will carry you through them and for the maturing, the Christlikeness He is going to achieve through them. Then in faith, thank Him as you count it all joy!

I Have Sinned. Again. Now What?

KAY

H ave you ever been tempted to sin?

      Were you a Christian? Did you yield? Did you have to?

Was there a way of escape that you didn't take? Were you sorry? What did you do? And if it involved another, did you make it right?

Ouch! Those are hard questions, aren't they? Ones you'd probably rather not answer. You can bury them…or deal with them. Numbers 32:23 warns us that our sins will find us out. Yes, I know this is an Old Testament passage, and I know we are under grace— grace that abounds beyond sin, as Romans 5:15-20 teaches. Grace, however, is never a license to sin; it is rather the power to say no to sin. (Paul covers that in Romans 6–8, but we're not going there. I just want you to know the address!)

HELP FOR THOSE IN A TRIAL

I want us to return to James 1 where we began yesterday as we looked at various trials, testings, and temptations that come our way. After introducing the subject of trials, James tells us how to gain the wisdom we need to get through the trial (1:5-8), then mentions how the humble and the rich are to look at them (1:9-11), and finally brings us to the blessing of those who persevere—who hang in there—through the trial. Then comes verse 12. I want you to read it for yourself:

> Blessed is a man who perseveres under trial; for once
> he has been approved, he will receive the crown of life
> which the Lord has promised to those who love Him.

Remember, trials show the genuineness of our faith. We're approved. It's life that awaits us. *A crown of life.*

But watch what follows verse 12, as James continues to deal with testings. As you read the text, color code or mark every occurrence of *tempted, tempt.*

13 Let no one say when he is tempted, "I am being tempted by God"; for God cannot be tempted by evil, and He Himself does not tempt anyone.

14 But each one is tempted when he is carried away and enticed by his own lust.

15 Then when lust has conceived, it gives birth to sin; and when sin is accomplished, it brings forth death.

Here we move from *peirasmos* to *peirazō*—from noun to verb. It means "to try, to prove in either a good or bad sense, tempt, test by soliciting to sin."[5] It is used of persons, to tempt, to prove, to put to the test.

Now, what do you learn from marking *tempted*? It's important that you see this for yourself, so list your insights below. Don't put down anything the text does not say—just the facts!

TRIALS AND TEMPTATIONS: WHAT'S THE DIFFERENCE?

In this context, the Spirit of God has moved James from trials and testings to temptation to sin. Read through the text again and mark *sin*. I color it brown. When you finish, list what you learn about sin. You may have already listed it, but do it again so you don't miss a thing. Careful, accurate observation is the key to correct interpretation, as well as to remembering that context rules in interpretation.

I have found James 1:13-15 to be an incredible picture of the workings of temptation and sin. Why does God deal with temptation—solicitation to do evil—right after dealing with trials? I believe He does that because many times in trials and tribulations we are tempted to get out of the trial our way rather than to persevere in it. For instance, how many people today are choosing divorce when marriage is difficult? Immorality when their hormones are hot? Abortion when they find out they're pregnant and having a child right then would be "inconvenient"?

We are not a culture that is strong in adversity—especially if it's personal adversity. We want to be comfortable, happy, and satisfied. Rather than being morally strong, we are sickeningly soft. For a great many, "It's all about me." That's why we sue tobacco companies, fast-food chains, and liquor stores. Our addiction or overindulgence has to be *their* fault; it couldn't be mine! We are even tempted to blame God.

But what does God say? "But each one is tempted when he is carried away and enticed by his own lust." God makes it clear we are tempted because of our *own* lust, our own desire.

Satan baits the hook with your favorite kind of worm or fills the trap with what you desire the most. "Entice" means to bait, hunt, trap. It's used for luring a fish out from under a rock. God is our rock. His name is Rock, and we are to stay "hidden in the cleft of the Rock." "Entice" is used for a hunter baiting a trap. You desire what's inside the trap, and instead of turning away because you know it's wrong, you go for it—and find yourself crushed in its jaws of iron or encased in a cage that won't let you free.

Just stop and think of the consequences of alcohol, drugs, or pornography. It's not pretty, is it? Any child, mate, or parent will tell you as much. It's destructive, disfiguring, disgraceful.

God makes that clear. When you follow your lust, sin is born, and when sin is brought to completion, it brings forth death.

What Gives Birth to Sin?

When I was in nurses training at St. Luke's Hospital in Cleveland, Ohio, I got on the elevator one day and looked at an African-American friend of mine from pathology. He was ashen. When I asked why, he told me what was wrapped up in his arms. It was a grossly deformed dead baby.

Whenever I read James 1:15, I think of that incident. *What are we giving birth to when we sin?* Did we get what we expected? Just think of all the Christian leaders who have yielded to sin. Did they think they would ever end up confessing their sin and airing their dirty laundry on national television before the world? Did they think about the death that would follow their actions? Death to a ministry, death to a good reputation, death to a hope, a dream, a calling...you add the rest.

Sin's Hidden Agenda

Is it really worth it? I've said it numerous times, but I will say it again: Sin will take you farther than you ever wanted to go, it will keep you longer than you ever intended to stay, and it will cost you more than you ever expected to pay. "Be sure your sins will find you out."

And to whom should we attribute that quote? God, of course. God who has already assured us that no temptation is more than we can bear. There is a way of escape. We simply choose not to take it (1 Corinthians 10:13).

So is all lost? We'll look at that in a minute, but before we do, it's important that you understand what God says is sin. Let's look at some key Scriptures. Since we are in James, we will begin with James 4:17. As you read each passage, underline what is defined as sin in the verse. If you want to, mark the word *sin*.

James 4:17

> Therefore, to one who knows the right thing to do and does not do it, to him it is sin.

Proverbs 21:2-4

> 2 Every man's way is right in his own eyes,
>
> But the LORD weighs the hearts.
>
> 3 To do righteousness and justice
>
> Is desired by the LORD more than sacrifice.
>
> 4 Haughty eyes and a proud heart,
>
> The lamp of the wicked, is sin.

Proverbs 24:9-10

> 9 The devising of folly is sin,
>
> And the scoffer is an abomination to men.
>
> 10 If you are slack in the day of distress,
>
> Your strength is limited.

Romans 14:23

> But he who doubts is condemned if he eats, because his eating is not from faith; and whatever is not from faith is sin.

1 John 3:4

> Everyone who practices sin also practices lawlessness; and sin is lawlessness.

1 John 5:17

> All unrighteousness is sin, and there is a sin not leading to death.

And what is the root of sin? I think Isaiah 53, that moving messianic chapter in the Old Testament, describes it well.

> 6 All of us like sheep have gone astray,
>
> Each of us has turned to his own way;
>
> But the LORD has caused the iniquity of us all
>
> To fall on Him.

THE ROOT OF SIN

The root of sin is choosing our way rather than God's. And what is "our way"? It is the path of unrighteousness, a lack of faith, pride, and rebellion. Couldn't you put all the verses that define sin under one of those words?

James further tells us that to sin really amounts to being *deceived*. In chapter 1, he continues:

16 Do not be deceived, my beloved brethren.

17 Every good thing given and every perfect gift is from above, coming down from the Father of lights, with whom there is no variation or shifting shadow.

Bottom line? "If it ain't good, it ain't from God!"

So now that you have read what God says is sin, what else do you need to know about it?

First, Jesus Christ is the propitiation for our sins (1 John 2:1-2). Do you remember that word and what it means? We looked at it much earlier. "Propitiation" means "covering, satisfaction for our sins."

We've looked previously at 1 John 2:1-2, but by way of review, do it again and mark the references to *sin* as you have before.

1 My little children, I am writing these things to you so that you may not sin. And if anyone sins, we have an Advocate with the Father, Jesus Christ the righteous;

2 and He Himself is the propitiation for our sins; and not for ours only, but also for those of the whole world.

So what do you learn from marking *sin*? List your observations.

Let's not stop there; there's something important to see as the text continues. Read 1 John 2:3-6 and color *know* green or put a box around it.

3 By this we know that we have come to know Him, if we keep His commandments.

4 The one who says, "I have come to know Him," and does not keep His commandments, is a liar, and the truth is not in him;

5 but whoever keeps His word, in him the love of God has truly been perfected. By this we know that we are in Him:

6 the one who says he abides in Him ought himself to walk in the same manner as He walked.

What do you learn from marking *know*? List your observations below.

Do you remember 1 John 3:4? "Everyone who practices sin also practices lawlessness; and sin is lawlessness." To be lawless is to break God's commandments. And how can you be sure, really sure, that you truly know Jesus, who is the propitiation for your sins? By *obeying* Him. By keeping His word.

According to 1 John 5:13, one of the key reasons John wrote this letter was so that you would *know* you have eternal life—that you truly are a child of God. You can also know by looking at your own lifestyle. It changes after you become a true child of God. Yes, you will still sin on occasion, as the Bible tells us. But instead of sin being a lifestyle, a habitual pattern you can't break, it happens on occasion when you take your eyes off of Jesus.

Listen to what God says in 1 John 3:7-10. As you read it aloud, mark the references to *sin*. You might also want to draw a red pitch-fork above *the devil*.

> 7 Little children, make sure no one deceives you; the one who practices righteousness is righteous, just as He is righteous;

> 8 the one who practices sin is of the devil; for the devil has sinned from the beginning. The Son of God appeared for this purpose, to destroy the works of the devil.

> 9 No one who is born of God practices sin, because His seed abides in him; and he cannot sin, because he is born of God.

> 10 By this the children of God and the children of the devil are obvious: anyone who does not practice righteousness is not of God, nor the one who does not love his brother.

Did you notice the word "deceives"? According to the text, what specific deception does God want you to avoid? Summarize it in your own words, as we will examine the text more closely in a minute.

The verb "practices" is in the present tense, which implies continuous action and habitual activity. In other words, a lifestyle. God says that if you are a child of His, you will not habitually practice sin. Instead, you will practice righteousness and live according to what God says. Again, does this mean you will never sin as a Christian?

Absolutely not! First John 2:1-2 addresses "little children," Christians, and John tells them he is writing so they will not sin. *Sin* is aorist tense—indicating a point in time, not something that is always present or habitual. But then God tells you that *when* you sin, you have an advocate—a lawyer, one called alongside to help—and it is Jesus!

A WAY OUT IS PROVIDED

Aren't you grateful—absolutely grateful that when you sin, it's not all over? Jesus is there. He paid for your sins in full and in doing so satisfied the holiness of God, and now He will come to your help. You do your part; He will do His.

And what is your part? It is to name your sin for what it is, to confess it to God. Listen carefully to 1 John 1:9, for these are practically the first words John pens on his parchment as he writes this letter. Mark any reference to *sins*.

> If we confess our sins, He is faithful and righteous
>
> to forgive us our sins and to cleanse us from all
>
> unrighteousness.

When we confess we don't whitewash sin. It's not, "Well, Lord, If I sinned..." No, we say, "God, I sinned! I _____ " (name my sin). Sin is sin and we call it so. And in doing so we agree with God. Then we know that because God is who He says He is—faithful and righteous—He will forgive that sin and (I love this) cleanse us from all unrighteousness, even those things we can't remember. Awesome! Because Jesus paid for all our sins and God is satisfied with the payment, in righteousness and remaining true to who and what He is, He forgives us.

When Jesus, then, teaches us *how* to pray (Matthew 6:9-15), He teaches us to ask for forgiveness of our sins *as* we have forgiven others. We must be willing to forgive others. If we refuse, that is sin, and God will not forgive us until we deal with it as sin. This is what Matthew 6:14-15; 18:21-35; and Ephesians 4:32 teach.

You can't rationalize it. You can't say, "But you don't know what was done to me. Surely you don't expect…"

I don't expect.

God does.

Don't argue with it, Beloved. You can't win. You are going against God, and that just doesn't work. It won't hold up in heaven's courts!

We have a dynamite 40-minute (no homework) Bible study on this whole subject: "Forgiveness: Breaking the Power of the Past." It is all Scripture and a powerful study for small groups, Sunday school, or family devotions. There are many good and helpful books written on forgiveness, but the one book that has been written on forgiveness that is pure truth is the Bible.

God's Book says it all. To not believe Him is sin—and it needs to be confessed as such.

And what is the precious by-product of confession? It's the comforting assurance that all is right between you and God because you did what God told you to do.

Now a word of caution: You need not do anything more, for to do so would be a lack of faith. You can't pay for your sin; the debt has been paid in full. Don't insult Jesus by imagining that you could somehow add to His sacrifice by your penance. It's not penance God wants; it's repentance. And that is what you do when you confess your sin, change your mind, and do what God says to do.

Now, if there is still no peace, it's probably just the devil tormenting you. Or perhaps there is still restitution or confession to be made to the one you violated. Leviticus 6:1-7 talks about restitution. If you borrowed, you return. If you stole, you pay back, even if it's a dollar at a time. If you lost, you restore. If someone gave you a deposit, you return it. If you transgressed against another human being, make it right to the best of your ability. Then you can look that person in the eye without guilt, and he will be more convinced that you truly are God's child.

Remember, nothing and no one is worth your peace with God and the knowledge that you are pleasing in His sight. As Paul did, make pleasing God your ambition (2 Corinthians 5:9). When you do, you'll feel His strength and be stronger for it.

Take Away

Ask God to search your heart. Is there anything in your life that is causing Him pain? If so, confess and forsake it. And then thank Him that you are truly forgiven.

Is There Any Help for My Sexual Temptations?

KAY

I find myself saddened, grieved, sickened, and greatly agitated at times with all the sexual immorality among those who profess to know Jesus Christ. The church, collectively, is pitifully weak in its knowledge of the whole counsel of God, in its giving, in its similarity to the world, and in the area of sexual purity.

As I study the Old Testament prophets, I gain a deeper understanding of how God felt about the licentious behavior of Israel, the nation to whom He betrothed Himself, the nation He referred to as His wife. Such knowledge makes me even more sensitive to the deep grief, the profound sorrow He must feel because of the one betrothed to His Son—the bride of Christ, the church.

ADULTERY HURTS THE HEART OF GOD

I think of God's words in Ezekiel, "How I have been hurt by their adulterous hearts which turned away from Me, and by their eyes which played the harlot after their idols, and they will loathe themselves in their own sight for the evils which they have committed, for all their abominations" (Ezekiel 6:9).

God's heart hurts. And the people of Israel in turn loathe themselves. No one wins. No one is satisfied. It is pain for both. How very, very sad. It isn't supposed to be this way.

Idolatry—the displacing of God with something else—leads to

immorality. You see it most clearly in Romans 1, although it is evidenced centuries before as Israel loses its fear of God and turns to idols and the immoral lifestyle that follows. When we turn away from the knowledge of God—the true knowledge of God and the fear of God that makes us feel accountable—eventually we lose our moral standards. With nothing restraining us, we become our own god, and our sexual desires then have free reign.

LOOKING TO FILL THE EMPTINESS WITH SEX

We think sex will somehow fill the void. We think about it (or about romance if we're a woman), dream about it, and eventually do it. But when it's not done God's way, it doesn't fill the void. Not really, not deeply. Instead it increases the emptiness.

When God made us, He designed us for reproduction and made it pleasurable. So very pleasurable, so strengthening to our health and well-being. Yet being the Creator and Designer of sex, He also knows the dangers of using it the wrong way. For this reason, He gave us clear commands: The sexual act is to be enjoyed only within the covenant of marriage; it's to be between only a man and a woman. Sex in any other way—same sex, family members, more than husband and wife, children, animals, and in the mind (pornography)—is wrong. It's sin. And you just saw that sin ends in death.

The commands are given not to spoil our fun or pleasure; they are to keep us from self-destructing sexually. When we go against God's will and break His commandments, our sexual appetite becomes like a well that can't be filled. Eventually we become sickened by our sin, weak and enslaved to an appetite that is always seeking some new thrill.

This is why Paul writes to the church in Thessalonica, urging them to excel still more in their walk with the Lord (1 Thessalonians 4:1) and reminding them of the commandments he gave them by the authority of the Lord Jesus Christ (4:2).

Did you notice the term "authority of the Lord"? "Lord" (kurios) means master. Jesus is never less than master because He is never less than God. Because He became man, He knows what it is to be tempted in every way we are tempted. But Jesus never yielded! He never acted apart from the will of God, and He wants the same for us. Remember, we are to be changed from image to image into His image (2 Corinthians 3:18; Romans 8:29). To see Jesus is to see the Father...and to see us should be to see Jesus.

God's Will?

So what is the will of God that Paul wants these Roman citizens to know and do? Do you remember the passage in 1 Thessalonians 4? I know you observed it days ago, but let's do it again. Review is good, and it will set the tone for the other passages I want us to look at. Read the following passage and underline *the will of God* or color it a color you won't miss.

> 3 For this is the will of God, your sanctification; that is, that you abstain from sexual immorality;
>
> 4 that each of you know how to possess his own vessel in sanctification and honor,
>
> 5 not in lustful passion, like the Gentiles who do not know God;
>
> 6 and that no man transgress and defraud his brother in the matter because the Lord is the avenger in all these things, just as we also told you before and solemnly warned you.
>
> 7 For God has not called us for the purpose of impurity, but in sanctification.
>
> 8 So, he who rejects this is not rejecting man but the God who gives His Holy Spirit to you.

Why would God have to write that to new believers? Because, Beloved, as it is in our world today, so it was in their world then. Sex outside of marriage was perfectly acceptable. Today what we deem immoral our culture embraces as moral—so acceptable it doesn't even have to be hidden. Do we hide sex outside of marriage? No, we announce it in the star-watcher tabloids and picture it on every visual media we can get it on, including the main piece of furniture in almost every home in America, the television.

SEX INFILTRATED EVERYWHERE

Immorality so reigned in the first century before Christ that it threatened the institution of marriage. Marriages became a "loose and voluntary compact [and] religious and civil rites were no longer essential."[6] People were obsessed with sex. It was part of the temple worship of their gods. Marital unions were so short-lived that Caesar Augustus enacted *lex Jusia de adulteriis,* "a law that tried to curb the people's addiction to widespread illicit sex."[7]

By the first and second centuries after Christ, marital faithfulness disappeared. People participated in all sorts of sexual methods, many absolutely obscene. They painted these practices without shame on their household objects—oil lamps, pitchers, plates, cups, bowls. This shameful lifestyle was practiced by the common man and by the emperors, so much so that *Qualis rex, talis grex* ("Like king, like people") became the cliché of the day. The debauchery was so great it became part of the entertainment at the palace. Incest, boy concubines, and many other perversions that I need not name were commonplace activities in the lives of Rome's leaders. Children were not shielded from such knowledge. It was part of the culture… of an empire that would soon fall!

This Roman culture of infidelity and immorality was without excuse. God had not left the empire without a witness. The One whom Rome crucified—the corn of wheat that fell into the ground and died—brought forth the fruit of many righteous followers. It was He, Jesus, who made it clear that adultery broke the sanctity of marriage. It was laid down from the beginning: "For this reason a man shall leave his father and his mother, and be joined to his wife; and they shall become one flesh" (Genesis 2:24). Paul would later write:

> Or do you not know that the one who joins himself to a prostitute is one body with her? For He says, "The two shall become one flesh." But the one who joins himself to the Lord is one spirit with Him. Flee immorality. Every other sin that a man commits is outside the body, but the immoral man sins against his own body. Or do you not know that your body is a temple of the Holy Spirit who is in you, whom you have from God, and that you are not your own? For you have been bought with a price: therefore glorify God in your body (1 Corinthians 6:16-20).

The early Christians understood this foundational truth—that their bodies were the temple of the Lord Jesus Christ. And it gave them great courage! They knew beyond all doubt that if they were martyred for their faith in Christ, they would immediately wake up in the presence of their Savior, the "better resurrection" spoken of in Hebrews 11:35. So confident were they in these truths that they were willing to resist every pressure of the culture—to come out and be separate and not touch the unclean thing—even if it cost them their lives. And for many, it did.

Because these believers stood against the godless, immoral trends of their time, Edward Gibbon writes, "The dignity of marriage was restored by the Christians."[8]

CHRISTIANS STOOD APART IN THEIR CULTURE

Galen, a Greek physician of the second century, was impressed with the upright sexual behavior of Christians. He said they were "so far advanced in self-discipline and...intense desire to attain moral excellence that they are in no way inferior to true philosophers."[9]

Christians of that day were a breed apart—a counterculture—as we are to be today. Isn't it sad that so often we fail in that calling? Instead of being a subculture, we become *submerged* in the culture! The very way many teens and some women dress belies holiness and puts such a stumbling block before men that many fight a constant battle because of what their eyes see and their manliness longs for. Yet if these men truly love God, they must be strong and must not allow themselves to be defrauded.

The ability to control our desires goes with salvation. Therefore, anyone who says, "I can't help myself; it's just who I am," and lives immorally is not truly born again. Don't be deceived into thinking you can live an immoral life and still go to heaven. Listen again to the words of God through Paul in 1 Corinthians 6:8-11:

> 8 On the contrary, you yourselves wrong and defraud. You do this even to your brethren.
>
> 9 Or do you not know that the unrighteous will not inherit the kingdom of God? Do not be deceived; neither fornicators, nor idolaters, nor adulterers, nor effeminate, nor homosexuals,
>
> 10 nor thieves, nor the covetous, nor drunkards, nor revilers, nor swindlers, will inherit the kingdom of God.
>
> 11 Such were some of you; but you were washed, but you were sanctified, but you were justified in the name of the Lord Jesus Christ and in the Spirit of our God.

Why don't you read that again and this time put a big red *S* over every sexual sin that is listed there. "Effeminate" carries the idea of effeminate by perversion (the NIV translates it "male prostitutes"). I think cross-dressers might also fit into this category.

What is the warning of verse 9? Write it out.

What do you learn from verse 11? What's the good news of that verse?

Don't you love the use of "were" in verse 11? Some of us *were* those things. But we who are truly His *were* washed—the blood of Jesus cleanses you and me from all sin. We—you, me, our brothers and sisters in Christ—*were* sanctified, set apart for God. We are not our own but blessedly His. We *were* justified, declared righteous because of Jesus' death and resurrection. He took our sin, and we received His righteousness (2 Corinthians 5:21). Our bodies are now His temples.

WHAT ABOUT YOU?

And what is the will of God regarding our sexuality? If you don't remember, go back and read 1 Thessalonians 4:3 again, aloud. Hear the voice of God—God your Father who desires your highest good; God your Father who will not give you more than you can bear and will always provide a way of escape. It is He who says, "Be holy, even as I am holy." Memorize that verse; it will come in handy just when you need it.

> For this is the will of God, your sanctification; that is, that you abstain from sexual immorality (1 Thessalonians 4:3).

Be strong. Learn, dear child of God, how to possess your body in holiness and in honor. Like Job, make a covenant with your eyes that you will not look on a woman to lust after her (Job 31:1). As Proverbs 5:19 says, be satisfied with the breasts of only your wife, if you are married. "Drink water from your own cistern." If you are single, don't be enticed by a woman on the make with her enticing words. Don't be a simpleton (Proverbs 7:7). Her bed is the way to hell (Proverbs 7:24-27). Tell her so...and walk away. Then find a godly woman to witness to her or send her a book. (You can send her mine: *The Truth About Sex*.[10] It has the gospel in it plus everything the Bible says about sex, including how to be forgiven and restored.)

Read Proverbs 5–7. If you are a man, don't let your springs be dispersed abroad (Proverbs 5:15-23). Your children should know who their father is and should be brought up in a home with their mother.

If you are a woman, remember it is the adulteress who hunts for the precious life. Don't reduce a man to the price of a loaf of bread (Proverbs 6:24-26). Don't dress like a harlot (Proverbs 7:10). You can't do that to God's temple and not go unjudged if you are truly God's daughter. You are to dress modestly and appropriately.

Be faithful to your husband—and remember that your body belongs to him, as his does to you. You are not to withhold sex from each other (I'm not talking about perversion, but God-designed and God-ordained physical oneness). Read 1 Corinthians 7:1-5. Live by it as a testimony to your love and obedience to God. It's a foolish woman who tears down her husband and her home.

I could write so much more on the subject of marriage, but it is already written in our Precept Upon Precept inductive study *Marriage Without Regrets* and in my book *A Marriage Without Regrets* (Harvest House Publishers). We also have two 40-minute Bible studies: "Building a Marriage that Lasts" and "What Does the Bible Say About Sex?"[11] Study them. Teach God's truths to others. Remember 2 Timothy 4:1-4:

1 I solemnly charge you in the presence of God and of Christ Jesus, who is to judge the living and the dead, and by His appearing and His kingdom:

2 preach the word; be ready in season and out of season; reprove, rebuke, exhort, with great patience and instruction.

3 For the time will come when they will not endure sound doctrine; but wanting to have their ears tickled, they will accumulate for themselves teachers in accordance to their own desires,

4 and will turn away their ears from the truth and will turn aside to myths.

TAKE AWAY

Whether you are male or female, when you are tempted, "2 Timothy 2:22 it": "Flee from youthful lusts and pursue righteousness." Run to the arms of Jesus, cry out for His help...then look at the nail prints in His hands. Remember, when you are truly His, you are willing to deny yourself, take up your cross, and follow Him as a habit of life for all of life.

Facing Death—What Should I Do?

KAY

Has the time come in America when we need to teach people not only how to live for Christ, but also how to die for Him? I think maybe so.

WHEN GIANTS OF THE FAITH PASS AWAY

I remember when two dear friends of mine, Bill Bright, the founder of Campus Crusade for Christ, and Brandt Gustavson, the president of the National Religious Broadcasters, were told—at about the same time—they didn't have long to live. Both determined they were going to show us and others how to die.

And they did. Both men died well. They knew what death for the Christian was all about, and this enabled them to be as strong in death as they were in life. And this, Beloved, is what David and I want for ourselves and for you.

News came just days ago telling us of Max Rondoni's homegoing. Max was a beloved Christian brother who, with his wife, ministered in Russia. We met them through the St. James Bible School in the Ukraine, a school established after the Iron Curtain came down in Russia. After many of our staff and Precept leaders taught there, Jack and I had the joy of also going to the school, meeting and teaching the students, and partnering with Max and Lois through our Russian Precept Bible studies.

Max was driving Joe Crockett of the American Bible Society to the San Francisco airport when he pulled to the side of the road, looked at Joe, and said, "I'm going to be with Jesus. Good-bye."

Max died instantly of a massive heart attack. What a way to go—in the midst of serving the Lord, with the name of Jesus on your lips!

Of course his family knows sorrow, but not as those who have no hope. His daughter wrote:

> My father and I went to lunch together (just a week before he died) at a place he especially loved. We never look at the menu. We have the same thing every time, a ritual at least two decades old. Our meal came, as perfect as it ever was, and we prayed Psalm 73:25, "Whom have I in heaven but you? I desire you more than anything on earth."

Do you suppose the apostles Peter, John, and Paul desired Jesus more than anything on earth? Of course! Their lives and their deaths bore witness to their great love of God.

What Impact Would It Have on You?

And what about you and me? If we desired God like this, how would death or the pronouncement of a death sentence strike us in our inner being?

"We got the report back, and I'm sorry to have to tell you that you have only months—perhaps weeks to live."

Or *"You must renounce your faith in Christ, or you will be executed tomorrow. What is your choice?"*

Yes, there are thoughts about death that are very troubling—particularly the manner of our dying. The apostle Peter knew how he would die because Jesus told him. After Jesus asked Peter three times if he loved Him, Jesus told him what his manner of death would be. It's recorded in John 21:18-22. Let's read it together. As you read it aloud, put a tombstone over any reference to *death*.

> 18 "Truly, truly, I say to you, when you were younger, you
> used to gird yourself and walk wherever you wished;

but when you grow old, you will stretch out your hands and someone else will gird you, and bring you where you do not wish to go."

19 Now this He said, signifying by what kind of death he would glorify God. And when He had spoken this, He said to him, "Follow Me!"

20 Peter, turning around, saw the disciple whom Jesus loved following them; the one who also had leaned back on His bosom at the supper and said, "Lord, who is the one who betrays You?"

21 So Peter seeing him said to Jesus, "Lord, and what about this man?"

22 Jesus said to him, "If I want him to remain until I come, what is that to you? You follow Me!"

In telling Peter he would die, Jesus also told him how it would happen...and it wouldn't be pleasant. Peter must have understood the "how," for there is no record of his asking Jesus what He meant when Jesus said, "You will stretch out your hands and someone else will gird you, and bring you where you do not wish to go." Tradition tells us Peter was crucified upside down.

And what did Peter want to know when Jesus told him this? *"What about John?"*

How did John die? All we know for sure is that he was exiled to the isle of Patmos in the Aegean Sea. Tradition tells us that he may have been immersed in a cauldron of hot oil before he was exiled. But it only disfigured him and didn't kill him.

And Paul? One thing we know for certain, as a Roman citizen,

Paul would not have been crucified. Tradition tells us he was beheaded. However his death came, it did not come as a surprise. Paul wrote to Timothy, his son in the Lord, that "the time of my departure has come" (2 Timothy 4:6), and he was confident "the Lord will rescue me from every evil deed, and will bring me safely to His heavenly kingdom" (2 Timothy 4:18).

Peter also knew the time of his departure was coming. Listen to what he writes in his final letter: "...knowing that the laying aside of my earthly dwelling is imminent, as also our Lord Jesus Christ has made clear to me" (2 Peter 1:14).

Did Peter, John, or Paul run from death? Beg? Plead for more days on the earth as King Hezekiah did (2 Kings 20)? There is no record of it. Rather it seems they embraced death, understanding that death for a child of God was different from the death of someone who did not embrace Jesus as the Son of God who takes away the sins of the world.

Peter and John were present when Jesus taught of two deaths and resurrections. In fact, John recorded it in his gospel. As you read the following passages, once again mark *death* with a black tombstone and color *life* yellow or put a big *L* over it.

John 5:24-29

24 "Truly, truly, I say to you, he who hears My word, and believes Him who sent Me, has eternal life, and does not come into judgment, but has passed out of death into life.

25 "Truly, truly, I say to you, an hour is coming and now is, when the dead will hear the voice of the Son of God, and those who hear will live.

26 "For just as the Father has life in Himself, even so He
gave to the Son also to have life in Himself;

27 and He gave Him authority to execute judgment,
because He is the Son of Man.

28 "Do not marvel at this; for an hour is coming, in
which all who are in the tombs will hear His voice,

29 and will come forth; those who did the good deeds to
a resurrection of life, those who committed the evil
deeds to a resurrection of judgment."

LIVING BREAD

John and Peter were also there with the other disciples in Capernaum when the multitude wanted to see another sign—wanted more bread and fish, like the miraculous feast Jesus had fed them the day before. More free food, like the manna God had fed their forefathers. Jesus instead offered them life.

Read the text and mark it as you did John 5.

John 6:48-51

48 "I am the bread of life.

49 "Your fathers ate the manna in the wilderness, and
they died.

50 "This is the bread which comes down out of heaven,
so that one may eat of it and not die.

51 "I am the living bread that came down out of heaven;
if anyone eats of this bread, he will live forever; and

the bread also which I will give for the life of the world
is My flesh."

Peter and John were also there when Jesus' friend Lazarus died, and Lazarus's sisters, Martha and Mary, questioned His late arrival. These two women were convinced that if Jesus had come earlier, He could have healed their brother.

John 11:23-26

> 23 Jesus said to her, "Your brother will rise again."
>
> 24 Martha said to Him, "I know that he will rise again in the resurrection on the last day."
>
> 25 Jesus said to her, "I am the resurrection and the life; he who believes in Me will live even if he dies,
>
> 26 and everyone who lives and believes in Me will never die. Do you believe this?"

DO YOU BELIEVE IT?

And so we come to Jesus' question, *Do you believe this?* Do you have faith that if you truly believe in Jesus—as God would have you believe—you will go on living even if you die? And if you live and believe in Him you will never die?

What is Jesus talking about? First, unless we live to see the return of Jesus Christ, all of us will experience physical death, even as Lazarus did. Our hearts will cease to beat, our lungs will cease to draw in oxygen. Yet if we believe in Jesus, we will simply pass from physical death to life eternal. We will not experience a second death, that of eternal separation from the Father, Son, and the Spirit in the lake of fire.

It is sin, Beloved, that separates us from God, that brings eternal separation, that gives Satan the power of death. However, if sin can be paid for in full, then Satan's power of death is broken. Listen to the writer of Hebrews:

Hebrews 2:14-15

> 14 Therefore, since the children share in flesh and blood, He Himself [Jesus Christ] likewise also partook of the same, that through death He might render powerless him who had the power of death, that is, the devil,
>
> 15 and might free those who through fear of death were subject to slavery all their lives.

Understanding the payment Jesus made for our sins, a payment that satisfied a Holy God—so much so that God would raise His Son from the dead, never to die again—ought to remove all fear of death. Death can't hold you in its grip if God holds you in His hand, as He says in John 10:27-29. With this in mind, Paul writes to Timothy, reminding him that Jesus abolished death and brought life and immortality to light. Read it, mark it, relish it.

2 Timothy 1:8-10

> 8 Therefore do not be ashamed of the testimony of our Lord or of me His prisoner, but join with me in suffering for the gospel according to the power of God,
>
> 9 who has saved us and called us with a holy calling, not according to our works, but according to His own purpose and grace which was granted us in Christ Jesus from all eternity,

10 but now has been revealed by the appearing of our

  Savior Christ Jesus, who abolished death and brought

  life and immortality to light through the gospel.

This perishable body will put on incorruption; this mortal body will put on immortality (1 Corinthians 15:53).

The First Martyr of the Church

We who believe will live forever in the presence of God. Stephen, the first of the deacons appointed by the apostles, knew this, and what Stephen knew he was willing to die for. Listen to what happens as he stands before the Sanhedrin and recounts for these religious rulers the history of Israel and Israel's unwillingness to listen to God.

Acts 7:54-60

> 54 Now when they heard this, they were cut to the quick, and they began gnashing their teeth at him.

> 55 But being full of the Holy Spirit, he gazed intently into heaven and saw the glory of God, and Jesus standing at the right hand of God;

> 56 and he said, "Behold, I see the heavens opened up and the Son of Man standing at the right hand of God."

> 57 But they cried out with a loud voice, and covered their ears and rushed at him with one impulse.

> 58 When they had driven him out of the city, they began stoning him; and the witnesses laid aside their robes at the feet of a young man named Saul.

> 59 They went on stoning Stephen as he called on the Lord and said, "Lord Jesus, receive my spirit!"

> 60 Then falling on his knees, he cried out with a loud

voice, "Lord, do not hold this sin against them!"
Having said this, he fell asleep.

Jesus stood at His Father's right hand, ready to receive Stephen into heaven, while Saul—who would very soon become the apostle Paul—stared at the robes of the witnesses of Stephen's stoning lying at his feet.

The death of Stephen didn't stop Paul. His zealous persecution of the church continued until God literally laid him low on the ground and saved him. God saved him; Jesus Himself taught him. It's recorded in Galatians 1:11-12: "For I would have you know, brethren, that the gospel which was preached by me is not according to man. For I neither received it from man, nor was I taught it, but I received it through a revelation of Jesus Christ." And so in his final letter, Paul would write to Timothy, "I know whom I have believed and I am convinced that He is able to guard what I have entrusted to Him until that day" (2 Timothy 1:12).

And what was Paul's passion? He tells us when he writes to the believers in Philippi: "According to my earnest expectation and hope, that I will not be put to shame in anything, but that with all boldness, Christ will even now, as always, be exalted in my body, whether by life or by death. For to me, to live is Christ and to die is gain" (Philippians 1:20-21).

To die is *gain*? Did we read that right? Gain?

Yes, gain. Since Paul said it, let's let him explain it. Hang on his every word. This is truth with a capital *T*! You may want to mark every reference to his body, such as *earthly tent* and *house*, with a stick figure.

2 Corinthians 5:1-6

> 1 For we know that if the earthly tent which is our
>
> house is torn down, we have a building from God, a
>
> house not made with hands, eternal in the heavens.

2 For indeed in this house we groan, longing to be clothed with our dwelling from heaven,

3 inasmuch as we, having put it on, will not be found naked.

4 For indeed while we are in this tent, we groan, being burdened, because we do not want to be unclothed but to be clothed, so that what is mortal will be swallowed up by life.

5 Now He who prepared us for this very purpose is God, who gave to us the Spirit as a pledge.

6 Therefore, being always of good courage, and knowing that while we are at home in the body we are absent from the Lord.

WHICH HOME WOULD YOU CHOOSE?

So which is better? Here or there? Earth or heaven? The company of men or of God? Of sinners or saints? Pain, suffering, conflict, and persecution or no more tears, pain, or death? Broken relationships and a hurting, wounded heart or no more sorrow? An aging, groaning, sagging body or an incorruptible, immortal, eternal body like the resurrection body of Jesus?

In all this we might be tempted to say, "But..." I think the *but* is only because we don't know better, or we can't begin to conceive just how good it will be "to be swallowed up by life"—real life.

Paul doesn't give us any details, but we do know he saw Paradise before he died. Listen to what he tells us of that experience in 2 Corinthians 12:2-4:

2 I know a man in Christ who fourteen years ago—
whether in the body I do not know, or out of the body
I do not know, God knows—such a man was caught
up to the third heaven.

3 And I know how such a man—whether in the body or
apart from the body I do not know, God knows

4 was caught up into Paradise and heard inexpressible
words, which a man is not permitted to speak.

In all probability this happened when Paul was stoned and left
for dead in Lystra (Acts 14:19-20). He tells us that "the surpassing
greatness of the revelations" (2 Corinthians 12:7) brought him a
thorn in the flesh, so that he wouldn't be overly puffed up by this
supernatural experience.

That is all we know of Paul's experience. Yet, there are things to
learn from it.

- We know he was caught up to the third heaven, and
  that's where Paradise is—up not down!

- We know that all this happened after the death, burial,
  and resurrection of Jesus Christ. Jesus had to be the first
  to be raised from the dead to die no more. The "firstborn from the dead" as Colossians 1:18 tells us "so that
  He might have first place in everything."

- We also know Paul saw things he was not permitted to
  speak—and he didn't.

If this experience happened when Paul was stoned at Iconium
on his first missionary journey, which occurred about A.D. 47–48,
Paul never even wrote about it until about A.D. 52–56, when on this
third missionary journey. He wrote to the Philippians during his
first imprisonment in Rome, which occurred about A.D. 60–62,
and expressed being hard-pressed from two directions: being with

Christ or remaining on this earth for the sake of the Philippians. His fondest desire shone through clearly: "To depart and be with Christ, for that is very much better" (1:23).

Not just "better," or even "much better," but *very much better*"! New Testament words like these are wonderful to think about if you find yourself facing death or the death of a loved one. And there may even come a day when you will be threatened with death if you continue to live for Jesus Christ.

Frightening as such prospects might be, you can cling to the hope that just around the corner, you and your loved ones in Christ will be living a life that is very, very, very much better than anything you have ever experienced.

STRONG IN THE FACE OF DEATH

So what do we know that can make us spiritually strong in the process of death?

First, though death is still an enemy, its power has been broken.

Second, death is like going to sleep and immediately waking up in heaven. Paul refers to death in these terms in 1 Corinthians 11:30; 15:6,18,20,51; and 1 Thessalonians 4:15-18.

Third, God Himself chooses the time of your passing, and you can't die without His permission. In Deuteronomy 32:39, God tells us. "It is I who put to death and give life." He numbers our days when there is not yet one of them (Psalm 139:16). The psalmist writes, "My times are in Your hand" (Psalm 31:15). In that you can rest, truly rest.

Fourth, you will be in God's presence—with His Son—seeing the place He has prepared for you, as He says in John 14:1-3.

Fifth, to die is to be absent from this body of failing flesh, and step into a new dwelling—a body from heaven. (Haven't you always wanted a heavenly body!)

Sixth, it is far better. Very much better.

D. James Kennedy, a faithful pastor, founder of Knox Seminary, and the father of the worldwide ministry of Evangelism Explosion, concurred. Listen to what he said:

Now I know that someday I am going to come to what some people will say is the end of this life. They will probably put me in a box and roll me right down here in front of the church, and some people will gather around and a few people will cry. But I have told them not to do that because I don't want them to cry. I want them to begin the service with the Doxology and end with the "Hallelujah Chorus," because I am not going to be there, and I am not going to be dead. I will be more alive than I have been in my life, and I will be looking down upon you poor people who are still in the land of the dying and have not yet joined me in the land of the living. And I will be alive forevermore, in greater health and vitality and joy than I have ever, ever known before.

Those words have been fulfilled. Dr. Kennedy departed to be with Christ in September 2007.

First Corinthians 15 is all about the resurrection and what it brings. It's awesome and well worth studying. First Thessalonians 4:13-18 tells us about the coming of Christ and the catching up of the saints, the rapture. But both of these indescribably wonderful chapters are for another time, another study.

TAKE AWAY

David and I want you to remember that "God has not destined us for wrath, but for obtaining salvation through our Lord Jesus Christ, who died for us, so that whether we are awake or asleep, we will live together with Him. Therefore encourage one another and build up one another, just as you also are doing" (1 Thessalonians 5:9-11).

Is There Victory over Fear?

DAVID

How are you doing, friend? Is it tough being a believer? Are you encountering the pains and struggles that come with being a Christian?

I'm sure it's different for different people. We all grow strong in the Lord on different schedules, don't we? The honeymoon period lasts longer for some than it does for others.

Today I want to discuss staying strong. I promise we will move on to more helpful activities to grow strong later on, but for now let's pause a moment and discuss perseverance.

MY FAVORITE STORY

One of my favorite stories in the Bible is found in Joshua 1. The setting of the story makes the promise and instruction God gives to Joshua come alive.

The setting: God has miraculously delivered the people of Israel out of the powerful hands of Pharaoh of Egypt. The people of Israel left Egypt with a promise in hand—a promise of land. After reaching the boundaries of the land and hearing the report of the 12 spies sent to check it out, they are devastated. Afraid. Full of doubt. Not sure that God is really trustworthy.

Why not?

Their intelligence report describes a land filled with giants—not friendly, dumb, storybook giants, but fierce warriors! The cities are well defended with walls too thick to penetrate.

Joshua 1 is the second attempt to enter the Promised Land. The first attempt failed miserably because the people refused to believe the promise that God would give them victory. So now, 40 years later, they stand at the boundary river again. Will they have faith in God this time?

Three times in just nine verses God tells Joshua to "be strong and courageous." That's an interesting instruction, isn't it? What is God saying here about the priority of His servants staying strong and keeping up their courage? Let's take a closer look at this question together.

LORD, HOW DOES THIS WORK?

So…how does that work, God? Am I supposed to find strength and courage on my own? Simply grit my teeth, clench my fists, and convince myself I *am* strong and I *am* courageous? Or is there something I'm missing?

I can remember going to the allergy doctor when I was about six years old. Back then allergy testing was more like a medieval torture than a medical procedure. I took off my shirt, baring my skinny little back, while the doctor stood waiting by the examining table with a tray full of sharp needles. After having me lie on my stomach, he pricked the skin all over my back with needle after needle after needle.

How did I make it through this ordeal? Had my mother urged me to "be strong and courageous"? If she said such a thing, I have no memory of it. What I do remember—quite clearly—were two promises that she made to me before the poking began. First, she said that it wouldn't hurt long; each prick would just sting for a moment. And second, she made the glorious promise that I would receive a lollipop for every single needle prick.

Every needle prick? There seemed to be a hundred. That meant a hundred lollipops! (It was probably more like 15 to 20, but it felt like a great treasure at the time.)

My point is simply this: The instruction to be strong and courageous was important, but it didn't stand alone. The instruction, the command, came with wonderful promises.

Let's look back at Joshua 1. Although the chapter is full of promises, I want to highlight just a few. Read the verse below and list everything God promises Joshua.

> "No man will be able to stand before you all the days of your life. Just as I have been with Moses, I will be with you; I will not fail you or forsake you" (Joshua 1:5).

God Is Everywhere All the Time— But He Promises to Be with Me?

What did God mean by saying, "I am with you?" Isn't God everywhere?

We have a word for that truth about Him; we say He is *omnipresent*—basically defined as "present everywhere." God is not confined to one space at a time like you and me. If I walk from the living room into my kitchen, I'm no longer in my living room. If I'm teaching a class in Atlanta, I'm no longer in Chattanooga. But God, because He is Spirit, is in the living room *and* my kitchen. He's present in Chattanooga, Atlanta, São Paulo, and Sidney, and with you at this very moment, wherever you may be. So what is He really saying when makes the promise, "I will be with you"? Isn't He always there?

One summer when I was about 11 or 12, I was visiting Florida with my family. Back then, I seemed to have a talent for finding trouble. I had found some boys who seemed to be a few years older and slightly bigger than me. My attempt to make friends backfired, and I found myself surrounded, being picked on.

I finally broke free from the mob and ran back to the house we were visiting. Mom and Dad weren't there, but my 17-year-old brother, Mark, was. I entered the house crying. You know the kind of crying that doesn't allow you to talk because the sobs are so deep?

Mark saw my tears and asked me, "Buddy, what's wrong?"

"Boys…boys…uhhh…beat me up."

Before I finished my explanation, Mark grabbed my arm, and we headed out the door and down the street. Mark was taking me back to the gang of boys who had just beaten me up!

But something was different. I wasn't scared anymore. I wasn't crying anymore. I was getting bolder and braver the closer we got to the gang. My chest began to swell with bravery, my eyes piercing the enemy like fiery darts.

What was the difference?

Mark was *with* me. Mark's presence was an assurance of strength, power, protection, and victory over my enemies.

God's promise to Joshua, "I will be with you," was the biggest and best promise God could ever make to him. God's presence meant God's favor, God's protection, God's provision—it meant God's power was on his side.

I've Got You—Don't Be Afraid

Look at another promise in verse 5. God said to Joshua, "I will not forsake you." What does that mean? On the surface it looks like a guarantee of something that had already been promised—God's presence. But the deeper we dig into this promise, the richer it becomes.

In the original Hebrew language, the word for "forsake" is the Hebrew word *raphah*. The Hebrews used this word to describe a slackening of one's grip on something. To *raphah* was to let go. Now take the visual image and put it back in the text. The promise was, "I will never forsake you." *Now* we understand the deeper dimensions of that promise; God was saying, "Joshua, I have you in My grip, and I won't slacken that grip for one moment."

When my oldest daughter, Jesse, was about three years old, we were looking at books in the downtown public library. Jesse was fascinated by all the books surrounding her, and I had a difficult time keeping her by my side while I was looking for a specific book.

Finally I stooped down to her level—eye to eye—and said these alarming words: "Jesse, there are people here who want to hurt you."

It may sound melodramatic, but it was true. And I was concerned for her. We were in a bad section of town, and the library was where the homeless came in during the winter to find warmth. The police were constantly escorting people out. Of course, not all the homeless people were dangerous, but some were.

What impact did my words have on my three-year-old daughter?

She gripped my arm as if she were holding on for dear life! She didn't let go the entire time we were in the library. She held on tight!

The roles changed once we left the library and crossed the busy four-lane road. At that point, I gripped her. Yes, she was holding on to me, but the grip that kept her safe was not her own—it was mine.

This is what God is promising Joshua. "I have you, son. Don't worry. I will be with you. But understand, no matter what, I will never, ever let you go. You are in My all-powerful grip!"

Without going into much detail to prove it, you need to understand that this promise is for you too. Romans 15:4 tells us clearly that the stories of the Old Testament are for our instruction and encouragement.

Paul writes to believers who suffered great persecution for their faith. In Romans 8 he describes the great comfort that comes from having assurance of God's love for His own.

Romans 8:35-39

35 Who will separate us from the love of Christ? Will tribulation, or distress, or persecution, or famine, or nakedness, or peril, or sword?

36 Just as it is written,

"For Your sake we are being put to death all day long; We were considered as sheep to be slaughtered."

37 But in all these things we overwhelmingly conquer through Him who loved us.

38 For I am convinced that neither death, nor life, nor angels, nor principalities, nor things present, nor things to come, nor powers,

39 nor height, nor depth, nor any other created thing, will be able to separate us from the love of God, which is in Christ Jesus our Lord.

Super-Duper Conquerors

I love the description of our victory in this passage. Paul doesn't simply say we will survive the attacks of the enemy; instead, he says we will *overwhelmingly conquer* through Him (Jesus) who loved us. Literally in the Greek, he calls the faithful Christian an über-conqueror—a superhero in the faith. Isn't that a reassuring picture of God's promise of protection? Look again and list out what Paul is convinced has no chance of separating us from the love of God in Christ Jesus our Lord.

The author of Hebrews also uses the story of God's promise to always be with Joshua to encourage his readers.

Make sure that your character is free from the love of money, being content with what you have; for He Himself has said, "I will never desert you, nor will I ever forsake you" (Hebrews 13:5).

The author of Hebrews is writing to Christians who suffered real heartbreak, trials, and persecution for their faith. He was writing to encourage them to endure, exercising faith in the Lord Jesus. He warned them about the dangers of drifting away from what they had previously been taught about the supremacy of Christ (2:1) and also warned them against a hardened and unbelieving heart (3:13-15):

13 But encourage one another day after day, as long as it is still called "Today," so that none of you will be hardened by the deceitfulness of sin.

14 For we have become partakers of Christ, if we hold fast the beginning of our assurance firm until the end,

15 while it is said,

"TODAY IF YOU HEAR HIS VOICE,

DO NOT HARDEN YOUR HEARTS, AS WHEN THEY PROVOKED ME."

God has made a promise to those who follow Him, to those who desire to grow strong in Him—a promise of a sure, never slipping, never slackening grip. God has you, my friend.

In light of that promise, He says to you, "Be strong and courageous." Does that help? Does it provide the strength and energy you need for persevering, for pressing on in your growth in the Lord?

TAKE AWAY

One of the biggest enemies of faith is fear. Fear has a way of distorting the truth. Fear can often cause you to stop growing strong spiritually. What will you do the next time fear sets into your heart?

Be strong and courageous. Exercise courage, knowing that God holds you with a grip that will not let you go. If you belong to God, then you can be completely confident that nothing and no one can ever take you from His grip of love.

Am I Supposed to Be Generous?

DAVID

He was the single largest stockholder of a very large company, and stocks had quickly dropped nearly 50 percent. Panic rang his doorbell, and fear pounded wildly on his door. *Will the stock continue to drop? Am I witnessing the beginning of the end of my wealth?*

But he knew what to do. He called his financial advisor with these firm instructions: "I need to increase my giving."

As you might imagine, his advisor was incredulous. "*What?* That's crazy! You don't need to increase your giving—you need to think about freezing your giving."

He told his advisor that for his own heart, he needed to give. He had begun to imagine that it was *his* money being lost. But it wasn't his money at all.

I can hear someone reply, "Oh, now I get it, David. I knew the other shoe had to drop sooner or later. Christians are always after my money. I turn on the TV and hear message after message from flashily dressed televangelists telling me to 'plant seeds of faith' in their ministries. The TV personality tells me that if I give, God will give back to me—in cash—tenfold, twentyfold, perhaps even a hundredfold. David, is that what you mean when you say it's good for a Christian to give? Is this some kind of racket that scoundrels posing as Christians dream up?"

No. Those types of people make me mad too. Actually, they make me sick to my stomach. I see them as wolves seeking helpless victims to devour with their deceptive messages. What I have to say in today's study has nothing to do with *them*. Instead, let's look at what Jesus has to say about our giving of our money, our stuff. Read the passage below and mark every reference to *treasure* with a dollar sign ($).

TREASURE STORED UP FOR YOU

Matthew 6:19-21

19 "Do not store up for yourselves treasures on earth, where moth and rust destroy, and where thieves break in and steal.

20 "But store up for yourselves treasures in heaven, where neither moth nor rust destroys, and where thieves do not break in or steal;

21 for where your treasure is, there your heart will be also."

What are we told *not* to do with our treasure?

What are we told to do with our treasure?

What are the reasons Jesus gives for not storing up treasures on earth?

How about the reasons for storing them in heaven?

According to verse 21, what is the "leader"? Is it your heart or your treasure? In other words, which one follows the other?

Don't Worry—Be Generous!

If you are a new Christian, giving might sound strange. You may wonder what will happen to you if you give of your treasures. How will you take care of your needs? What about saving as much as you can for the future?

Let's keep reading in Matthew 6 to see what else we can learn about giving. Specifically see what you can learn about worrying about your needs. As you read this time, circle every mention of *worry* or *worried*.

> 24 "No one can serve two masters; for either he will hate
> the one and love the other, or he will be devoted to
> one and despise the other. You cannot serve God and
> wealth.
>
> 25 "For this reason I say to you, do not be worried about
> your life, as to what you will eat or what you will
> drink; nor for your body, as to what you will put on.
> Is not life more than food, and the body more than
> clothing?

26 "Look at the birds of the air, that they do not sow, nor reap nor gather into barns, and yet your heavenly Father feeds them. Are you not worth much more than they?

27 "And who of you by being worried can add a single hour to his life?

28 "And why are you worried about clothing? Observe how the lilies of the field grow; they do not toil nor do they spin,

29 yet I say to you that not even Solomon in all his glory clothed himself like one of these.

30 "But if God so clothes the grass of the field, which is alive today and tomorrow is thrown into the furnace, will He not much more clothe you? You of little faith!

31 "Do not worry then, saying, 'What will we eat?' or 'What will we drink?' or 'What will we wear for clothing?'

32 "For the Gentiles eagerly seek all these things; for your heavenly Father knows that you need all these things.

33 "But seek first His kingdom and His righteousness, and all these things will be added to you.

34 "So do not worry about tomorrow; for tomorrow will care for itself. Each day has enough trouble of its own."

Look at your markings of *worry* and *worried* and answer the following questions:

What things are we told not to worry about?

What reasons does Jesus give us to not worry?

How Do I Let Go?

Giving is often connected to worrying. The image can either be an open hand or a closed fist. Giving is the open hand while worrying is the clenched fist. So how do we go from clenched fist to open hand with our treasures?

Jesus tells us first in verse 24 that we have to choose a master. The choice is either God or wealth—but not both. A master decides your agenda, your life. God and wealth are competitors for your life, and Jesus says that to try to love them both is futile. It simply won't work. Either you will love God—alone—or you will hate Him.

Hate God?

Why must I choose? Why can't I love them both?

Jesus answers this question in verse 21. Our treasure points directly to that which controls our hearts. If your treasure points toward yourself—your wants, your needs, your plans, your dreams and desires—then that's an indicator. You are devoted to yourself and yourself alone. But if your treasure is pointed toward God, then your heart will follow.

I can prove it.

Let's say your sweet grandmother passes away at a ripe old age and leaves you a fortune in her will. A fortune! "Yes!" you say. "Now

I can buy that dream home, education, or (in my case) that fully loaded, Ford F-350 Crew Cab, 4x4—shiny black!" But your financial advisor talks you into investing all of your money into Microsoft. All of it. Every penny. In fact, it's such a great buy that you take all the other funds you have and invest them in Microsoft. Your treasure is invested in the company Bill Gates owns.

Do you think that when you hear about Bill Gates on TV your attention will be captured? Or if you see in the paper that Bill is acting crazy, your worry level will increase? Why is that? Because your treasure has led your heart into Microsoft. Your attention, passion, and concern is with Microsoft because you have your treasure there. Jesus said it—where your treasure is, there your heart will be also.

KINGDOM SEEKING AND MY DILEMMA

Did you notice verse 33? "But seek first His kingdom and His righteousness, and all these things will be added to you."

For years I struggled in my soul every time I attended a missions conference. I would ask God, *Am I supposed to be a missionary? God, do You want me to seek first Your kingdom?* This happened when I was in high school and college and even continued into my business career with IBM.

But then I went into full time ministry. I went to seminary, became a pastor, and committed my weeks to "seeking first the kingdom." The guiltlike feelings went away at the next missions conference and stayed away.

I had convinced myself that I was now obeying Matthew 6:33 and seeking first His kingdom...until I studied this passage and noted the context of the verse. The context can be determined by simply reading the verses before and after a specific passage. Once I realized the context was about my money, my treasure, I knew something had to change. I finally came to this conclusion: To "seek first His kingdom" meant placing my treasure in the work of that kingdom and not get caught up in worrying about earthly investments. And as recent events in the stock market and our nation's economy have shown us, there's really no such thing as a "safe investment" on this earth.

More Confessions from David, the Tickled Tither

I had become content with giving my tithe. You know, giving ten percent of my income to the church. I heard a similar testimony from Pastor Bob Coy of Calvary Chapel, Fort Lauderdale, Florida. Bob said he was a "Tickled Tither," and I could relate.

In other words, I was pleased with myself (tickled) because I was obeying the Bible with my giving. But was I really? When I explored the tithe, which was initiated in the Old Testament, I discovered that there were two annual tithes and one tithe that occurred every three years. Do the math. That comes out to 23.3 percent—much more than the meager 10 percent I had been giving. I confess that I still struggle with giving generously—giving more than the tithe. It's a process, a journey that even a guy like me who has been a Christian for more than 28 years still needs to grow in.

So exactly how much should a Christian give?

There is no direct answer in the Bible. Even in the Old Testament where the tithe was required, there were still instructions about freewill offerings. Freewill gifts were above and beyond the tithe. A precise amount, though, was never dictated to the people of God.

An Unbelievable Story of Generosity

Let's look at a passage in the New Testament where the apostle Paul is collecting an offering for the church in Jerusalem. He's asking for an offering from the churches that he planted throughout Asia. In the passage below we find Paul talking to the Corinthian church about their participation in this offering. To encourage them to give generously, he shares with them about another church that gave to the effort. This church is amazing!

As you read this passage, mark every mention of *give*, *gave*. Also mark *liberality* in the same manner. "Liberality" can also be translated "generosity."

2 Corinthians 8:1-5

1 Now, brethren, we wish to make known to you the grace of God which has been given in the churches of Macedonia,

2 that in a great ordeal of affliction their abundance of joy and their deep poverty overflowed in the wealth of their liberality.

3 For I testify that according to their ability, and beyond their ability, they gave of their own accord,

4 begging us with much urging for the favor of participation in the support of the saints,

5 and this, not as we had expected, but they first gave themselves to the Lord and to us by the will of God.

According to verse 1, what role did God play in the giving of the churches of Macedonia?

According to verse 5 where did the giving of the Macedonian church begin?

Read verse 2 again. What was the condition of the Macedonian church?

What was the result of their deep poverty? Try to use words in the text to answer this question.

What is going on here? How can a church give beyond its ability (v. 3)? Isn't it incredible to see the role that the grace of God plays in our life? In our giving?

Let's continue to read in 2 Corinthians. As you read this passage, mark every mention of *supply, supplies,* and *liberality,* the same as you marked *giving* earlier.

2 Corinthians 9:10-15

> 10 Now He who supplies seed to the sower and bread for food will supply and multiply your seed for sowing and increase the harvest of your righteousness;
>
> 11 you will be enriched in everything for all liberality, which through us is producing thanksgiving to God.
>
> 12 For the ministry of this service is not only fully supplying the needs of the saints, but is also overflowing through many thanksgivings to God.
>
> 13 Because of the proof given by this ministry, they will glorify God for your obedience to your confession of the gospel of Christ and for the liberality of your contribution to them and to all,

14 while they also, by prayer on your behalf, yearn for

you because of the surpassing grace of God in you.

15 Thanks be to God for His indescribable gift!

WHO GIVES TO WHOM?

Who supplies the seed? God does. What does God promise in supplying the seed? Paul says God will *multiply* your seed, *increase* the harvest of your righteousness. So what does giving to the saints accomplish besides meeting their needs? Verse 12 tells us that it overflows in thanksgiving to God. Our giving glorifies God!

Look again at verses 12 and 13. What do you think "the ministry" is in this context? What is the result of this ministry, according to verses 13-15?

Now read what Paul says in 9:6-7:

6 Now this I say, he who sows sparingly will also reap sparingly, and he who sows bountifully will also reap bountifully.

7 Each one must do just as he has purposed in his heart, not grudgingly or under compulsion, for God loves a cheerful giver.

So how much should a Christian give? We are to give or sow the seed, which the Sower (God) has given us, generously. According to verse 7 we are to give from the heart. And as we learned earlier, the heart will follow the treasure.

Finally, we see in verse 7 that God loves a cheerful giver. A cheerful giver is one who understands that God is the true giver and that their giving is a ministry, an act of worship to God, bringing Him glory.

Take Away

When you and I give to the Lord, we're acting as funnels of what has never really belonged to us in the first place. In His grace and kindness, He gives us the opportunity (and the joy!) to funnel His good gifts to others in need. But our own lives are blessed beyond measure as the treasure passes through our hands. Remember what Jesus said? "Give and it will be given to you!" But far, far beyond any consideration of God's material gifts, we have the gift of Jesus Himself—heaven's most precious treasure.

Close out the day by meditating on the verse below and thanking God for His generous gift that saved your life:

2 Corinthians 8:9

> For you know the grace of our Lord Jesus Christ, that though He was rich, yet for your sake He became poor, so that you through His poverty might become rich.

Do I Have a Spiritual Gift?

David

Where do I fit? This might be your question. How do I, a new believer or perhaps a struggling believer, fit into the family of Christ? As I look to the superstars in my church, I wonder if I will ever be a great teacher or leader or servant. Maybe you are thinking it would be best to just stay to yourself and not get involved or commit yourself to the people of the church.

In my role as a pastor, I heard this expressed many times and in many different ways. I recognize that it's all too easy to simply attend church as one attends a play or movie. You can slip in and out of many churches without even being noticed, let alone becoming truly connected to the family of Christ that worships there. But is this okay? Is it okay to simply work on your own spiritual growth, by yourself and for yourself?

Today I want to show you some amazing pieces of Scripture. This first passage comes from the apostle Paul. Paul was a church planter, who saw his role as preaching the gospel of Jesus Christ. As people were converted to Christ, he quickly went about the business of equipping them to work together as a body.

The first passage I want us to consider together is 1 Corinthians 12:1-11. Paul wrote this letter to one of his church plants, the church in Corinth. This letter seems to be arranged topically, dealing with issues in the church and answering questions the church was struggling with.

SPIRITUAL GIFTS

The topic Paul addresses in 1 Corinthians 12 is spiritual gifts. A spiritual gift is what the Holy Spirit gives to each and every Christian at the time he or she becomes a believer. Even though the Holy Spirit gives different gifts to different Christians, the gifts are not designed to make different classes of Christians. Spiritual gifts are designed to build up or edify the body of Christ (Ephesians 4:16).

Read the text below and mark every mention of *gift* or *given* as well as every mention of *the Holy Spirit*.

1 Corinthians 12:1-11

1 Now concerning spiritual gifts, brethren, I do not want you to be unaware.

2 You know that when you were pagans, you were led astray to the mute idols, however you were led.

3 Therefore I make known to you that no one speaking by the Spirit of God says, "Jesus is accursed"; and no one can say, "Jesus is Lord," except by the Holy Spirit.

4 Now there are varieties of gifts, but the same Spirit.

5 And there are varieties of ministries, and the same Lord.

6 There are varieties of effects, but the same God who works all things in all persons.

7 But to each one is given the manifestation of the Spirit for the common good.

8 For to one is given the word of wisdom through the Spirit, and to another the word of knowledge according to the same Spirit;

9 to another faith by the same Spirit, and to another gifts of healing by the one Spirit,

10 and to another the effecting of miracles, and to another prophecy, and to another the distinguishing of spirits, to another various kinds of tongues, and to another the interpretation of tongues.

11 But one and the same Spirit works all these things, distributing to each one individually just as He wills.

What do you see the Holy Spirit doing in this passage? Make a list below.

What do you learn from marking *gifts* and *given*?

Did you notice the variety of gifts but the unity of the Spirit? How do the gifts make us both unique and unified?

BODY TALK

Read through the rest of the chapter and draw a little stick figure over every mention of *body*, and circle every mention of *member(s)*.

12 For even as the body is one and yet has many members, and the members of the body, though they are many, are one body, so also is Christ.

13 For by one Spirit we were all baptized into one body, whether Jews or Greeks, whether slaves or free, and we were all made to drink of one Spirit.

14 For the body is not one member, but many.

15 If the foot says, "Because I am not a hand, I am not a part of the body," it is not for this reason any the less a part of the body.

16 And if the ear says, "Because I am not an eye, I am not a part of the body," it is not for this reason any the less a part of the body.

17 If the whole body were an eye, where would the hearing be? If the whole were hearing, where would the sense of smell be?

18 But now God has placed the members, each one of them, in the body, just as He desired.

19 If they were all one member, where would the body be?

20 But now there are many members, but one body.

21 And the eye cannot say to the hand, "I have no need of you"; or again the head to the feet, "I have no need of you."

22 On the contrary, it is much truer that the members of the body which seem to be weaker are necessary;

23 and those members of the body which we deem less honorable, on these we bestow more abundant honor, and our less presentable members become much more presentable,

24 whereas our more presentable members have no need of it. But God has so composed the body, giving more abundant honor to that member which lacked,

25 so that there may be no division in the body, but that the members may have the same care for one another.

26 And if one member suffers, all the members suffer with it; if one member is honored, all the members rejoice with it.

27 Now you are Christ's body, and individually members of it.

28 And God has appointed in the church, first apostles, second prophets, third teachers, then miracles, then gifts of healings, helps, administrations, various kinds of tongues.

29 All are not apostles, are they? All are not prophets, are they? All are not teachers, are they? All are not workers of miracles, are they?

30 All do not have gifts of healings, do they? All do not

speak with tongues, do they? All do not interpret, do they?

31 But earnestly desire the greater gifts. And I show you a still more excellent way.

What do you learn from marking *body* and *members*? Record your observations below:

Body   **Members**

Did you notice God's role in all of this? Write your observations below.

Up to this point in the passage Paul had been talking about the unity of believers. He told them they were one body. But Paul wants to clarify that they are not all alike. In verse 14 we see that the body— or the group of believers in the individual churches—is not just one member but many members. Paul then illustrates with the human body that we are different from one another and yet need each other to live.

CHURCH OR CLIQUES?

Do you remember high school? (You may even be there right now.) Have you ever noticed how people seem to hang out with those who look like they do? At my school there were cliques—groups of students who had something in common. The cliques were easily identified. You remember the saying, "Birds of a feather flock together"? The athlete types (we called them jocks) all looked alike: strong, fast, big. They could usually be spotted easily because they were all wearing their letter jackets or team jerseys.

Then there was the artistic bunch. They were easily defined due to their strange attire. Crazy, mismatched clothes in clashing colors and patterns.

The academic types also had a clique. You could usually find them with their noses in a book or at a computer.

Of course every school had the popular and pretty crowd.

I'm having flashbacks as I write this. I wasn't in any of those groups when I was in high school. I did letter in soccer and was even the team captain my senior year, but I didn't hang with the jocks. Since I'm neither artistic, intelligent, or particularly good-looking, I didn't run with those groups. No, I had to start my own. We were the Quids. Don't ask how we named ourselves, we just did. We became known as the funny crowd—the ones most likely to get in trouble because of pranks pulled on other students. I guess we were the collection of class clowns.

God's idea for the church is different from the exclusive cliques of high school. We learn in verse 18 that God shapes the body by combining different members together. Actually, the gifts and giving of them are decided by God. We learn from the context of this passage that it is God the Holy Spirit who puts the different members together to make one body.

Do You Know Yet Where You Belong?

So where do you fit? What gift or gifts do you think the Lord has given you?

This may not come to you right away. It may not be obvious the moment you join a church, but give it time. Ask the Holy Spirit to show you what part of the body of Christ you are to be in your local church. It's also a good idea to talk to the leaders of your church and ask how you can serve the body.

The New Testament is packed full of passages about believers interacting with one another and using their gifts. But it's not just gifts that make us fit in the church. Most of the New Testament letters speak about serving one another, forgiving one another, loving one another. The phrase "one another" appears again and again.

The second passage we will look at is one of my favorites. This passage is found in Paul's letter from prison to one of his church plants, Philippi. In this letter the apostle teaches about a joy that can be found in the midst of pain, struggle, and even betrayal.

As you read Paul's teaching about connection or fellowship within the body of Christ, put a circle around any of the words that communicate *unity, oneness, sameness.*

Philippians 2:1-4

1 Therefore if there is any encouragement in Christ, if there is any consolation of love, if there is any fellowship of the Spirit, if any affection and compassion,

2 make my joy complete by being of the same mind, maintaining the same love, united in spirit, intent on one purpose.

3 Do nothing from selfishness or empty conceit, but with humility of mind regard one another as more important than yourselves;

4 do not merely look out for your own personal interests, but also for the interests of others.

According to verse 2, what completes Paul's joy?

How do verses 3 and 4 lead to what Paul is looking for in verse 2?

I have often thought that if the Christian community took verse 4 seriously and sought to obey it consistently, we would shine the light of Christ in a way beyond our imagination. Just imagine what might happen if all the people in your church did *everything* in the interest of others! Can you even imagine the impact that would have on our world? What would society look like if we lived such lives of humility that we were always eager to regard others as more important than ourselves? I think we would have a whole lot fewer attorneys and policemen.

But how can we do this? Can it be done? Or is this some type of imaginary Christian utopia? Paul's answer to this question should blow us out of the water.

Philippians 2:5-8

> 5 Have this attitude in yourselves which was also in
> Christ Jesus,
>
> 6 who, although He existed in the form of God, did not
> regard equality with God a thing to be grasped,
>
> 7 but emptied Himself, taking the form of a bond-
> servant, and being made in the likeness of men.
>
> 8 Being found in appearance as a man, He humbled

Himself by becoming obedient to the point of death,

even death on a cross.

Attitude describes our way of thinking, believing, and processing information and desires. According to this passage, all of it—every bit of it—should reflect the attitude of Christ. Christ put aside His right of being on the throne with His Father. Instead of sitting on the throne, He took on the role of a servant—a servant who gave His life on the cross for you and me.

What standard of love are we to show to one another? Does God just want us to get along—you know, what Dad desired for us kids on long road trips? In John 13, Jesus demonstrated the kind of love we are to have for one another. He washed His disciples' feet, the act of the most humble of servants. In verses 34-45, He describes the standard of love we should have for one another:

> 34 "A new commandment I give to you, that you love one
> another, even as I have loved you, that you also love
> one another.
> 35 "By this all men will know that you are My disciples,
> if you have love for one another."

Wow. We are to love one another just as Christ loves us!

Without Christ it is impossible to be one, united in spirit and purpose. Our fellowship, then, is simply living out the attitude of our Savior in the giving of ourselves to one another.

It means you truly *do* have a place in the body, a role to fill, a purpose to commit to. God has shaped you uniquely, and through the Spirit He will place you into the role He designed for you. He has not called you to be a member of a clique but a member of one body, the church.

TAKE AWAY

If you are a born again believer, the Holy Spirit has customized you for service. He has granted you a special gift to serve the brothers and sisters in Christ. What is it? What is your gift to use for serving one another? How do you plan to use this gift in your fellowship of believers? Where can you fit best in your church?

Take some time to think and pray about these questions. Perhaps ask another believer who knows you well what they see in you as a gift from the Holy Spirit.

Day 26

Does God Still Like the Church? Why?

DAVID

I had been working for Precept Ministries for nearly five years when it happened. Within just a few weeks I received an offer to attend seminary, work in a great church, and pursue a master's degree in theology. It was a God-thing.

In seminary, I must have looked like a kid in a candy store with a wad of cash in my hand. I was so excited to be able to study in depth and in community. This is where my love for the church caught fire. I realized that the church was not man's idea but God's.

Growing up on the campus of Precept Ministries in the seventies was fun. We lived on a large ranch in this lush green valley. There were always people of all ages and from all walks of life living there besides my family. Many nights we ate dinner together—anywhere from a dozen folks up to 30. It really was an extended family.

"Wait," someone may say. "Doesn't that sound a little like a cult?"

Trust me, it wasn't. Everyone had their own possessions and ideas; this was not a compound or a commune. So what was it? It was a body. A wonderful and beautiful collection of brothers and sisters in Jesus. Young, old, black, white, rich, and poor.

On Sundays, we dispersed around Chattanooga and attended different churches—some Baptist, some Methodist, some, like my family, Presbyterian.

SO WHAT IS CHURCH?

First, we should see how it all began. The history of the church is recorded in the book of Acts—and covers way too much territory for the scope of this book. But I want you to see God's role in building the church. If you recall, the Bible was originally given to the Jews, the children of Abraham, Isaac, and Jacob. They were known as Hebrews or Israelites. They weren't the biggest people group on the planet, nor were they the most powerful. But God set His love and affection on them and made a promise that He would be their God and they would be His people.

So where does that leave the rest of the world? The Bible divides people into two basic groups—Jews and Gentiles.

Abraham, you could say, is the father of the Jews. We read in Genesis 12:3 about the promise, also known as a covenant, that God made with Abraham.

> "And I will bless those who bless you, And the one
>
> who curses you I will curse. And in you all the fami-
>
> lies of the earth will be blessed."

In Abraham, God would bless not just the Jews but all the families of the earth. He explains it a bit more in Genesis 22:17-18:

> 17 "Indeed I will greatly bless you, and I will greatly
>
> multiply your seed as the stars of the heavens and as
>
> the sand which is on the seashore; and your seed shall
>
> possess the gate of their enemies.
>
> 18 "In your seed all the nations of the earth shall be
>
> blessed, because you have obeyed My voice."

God tells Abraham that He will bless all the nations (Jew and Gentile) through Abraham's seed. This must have been a strange—and surprising—bit of news for Abraham to hear. You see, Abraham was an old man, more than a hundred years old. Not only was he old, but he and his wife Sarah had only one son who was the son of the promise, Isaac (Genesis 17:21). And even stranger than that, God had just told him to—literally—offer up Isaac as a sacrifice to God.

The Lord Himself, however, stopped Abraham before he could plunge a knife into the chest of his much-loved son. It had been a test of the old man's devotion, and he had passed with flying colors. It would indeed be through Isaac that God would multiply Abraham's descendants like the stars, and bless all the nations of the earth. The rest of the story in the Old Testament focuses on God working with Abraham's descendants, the people of Israel.

Are Gentiles a Part of the Body?

But what about the Gentiles?

Paul describes the building of the church in Ephesians 2:11-22. He shows how the Jew and the Gentile, once separated, are now brought together into a unified body, the church. The "you" in this passage refers to Gentile believers, since they are the ones Paul was writing to.

Circle every mention of the *Gentile Christians* and put a Star of David like this ✡ over every mention of *Israel, the circumcised, those who were near* (verses 11-12,17), and *the saints* (verse 19).

Ephesians 2:11-22

> 11 Therefore remember that formerly you, the Gentiles in
> the flesh, who are called "Uncircumcision" by the so-
> called "Circumcision," which is performed in the flesh
> by human hands—
>
> 12 remember that you were at that time separate from
> Christ, excluded from the commonwealth of Israel,
> and strangers to the covenants of promise, having no
> hope and without God in the world.

13 But now in Christ Jesus you who formerly were far off have been brought near by the blood of Christ.

14 For He Himself is our peace, who made both groups into one and broke down the barrier of the dividing wall,

15 by abolishing in His flesh the enmity, which is the Law of commandments contained in ordinances, so that in Himself He might make the two into one new man, thus establishing peace,

16 and might reconcile them both in one body to God through the cross, by it having put to death the enmity.

17 And He came and preached peace to you who were far away, and peace to those who were near;

18 for through Him we both have our access in one Spirit to the Father.

19 So then you are no longer strangers and aliens, but you are fellow citizens with the saints, and are of God's household,

20 having been built on the foundation of the apostles and prophets, Christ Jesus Himself being the corner stone,

21 in whom the whole building, being fitted together, is growing into a holy temple in the Lord,

22 in whom you also are being built together into a

dwelling of God in the Spirit.

What did you learn about the condition, the situation, of the Gentile prior to Jesus?

Read through this passage again, and this time mark every reference to *Jesus* or *Christ* (don't miss the pronouns). Did you notice the phrase "*in* Christ"? What do you see happen to those "*in* Christ"? What is the end result?

A Living and Breathing Building

Do you see the references to this "building," this "holy temple"? This is no ordinary building, constructed of brick and mortar. Rather, it is made up of *people*—Jewish and Gentile believers in Jesus, one new man!

When the overwhelming reality of what Christ had built—the church—finally settled in my mind, it made a lasting impact on my life. From that day forward I committed my life to serving the church. Sensing the Lord's call to serve His church, I went from seminary to the pastorate.

Now, a decade later, I'm no longer a full-time pastor. I serve now full-time with Precept Ministries, but my calling is still to serve the church, the body of Christ. We love the church at Precept. In fact, we placed Her in our mission and vision statement: "Our mission is to establish people in God's Word, and our vision is to see people living as exemplary followers of Christ, studying the Bible inductively, viewing the world biblically, making disciples intentionally and *serving the church* faithfully in the power of the Holy Spirit."

(By the way, I'm still a part-time assistant pastor at my church. My annual salary is one dollar. Some of the congregation joke with me that I'm overpaid!)

What should you do as a believer? Go to church. There you will see the different members of the body—arms, legs, eyes, mouths—all different but all serving together. There you will experience the "growing temple," an organism, not an organization. The church is dynamic, alive, real.

I will admit that not all churches are healthy and growing. What might the problem be? How could it be addressed? Could it be that they need someone like you? Someone with the gifts that the Holy Spirit has given to you to use in the building up of the church? Someone to love and serve "one another"?

TAKE AWAY

You are not alone. You are never alone. The One who indwells you has shaped and placed you in the body of Christ made up of believers everywhere (Church with a capital C). He also desires for you to be a part of a local body of believers (church with a lowercase c). Take some time today to evaluate your role in your local church. How are you serving one another? What opportunities are waiting for you to get involved?

Meditate on what you have learned. Use this passage as a prayer for yourself and for your church—and then watch God work!

Romans 15:5-6

> 5 Now may the God who gives perseverance and
>
> encouragement grant you to be of the same mind with
>
> one another according to Christ Jesus,

> 6 so that with one accord you may with one voice glo-
>
> rify the God and Father of our Lord Jesus Christ.

Don't Walk by Sight? Then How?

DAVID

"You've just got to have faith!"

What does that statement really mean? Is faith some kind of Christianized word to describe crossing your fingers, squeezing your eyes shut tight, and hoping it all works out? Do you have faith in something—or someone? Is faith available only to Christians, or do all religions have faith?

FAITH IN A BOAT

Let's start with a story about faith in Mark 4:35-41. As you read, mark every reference to *Jesus*. Also mark every reference to the people Jesus is addressing—the disciples. And since we're talking about *faith*, mark that word as well. If you have some colored pencils, try using different colors to mark these references. This will make them stand out on the page. If you do this in your Bible, it will make it easy to find different key words you have already marked. I mark *faith* in blue in my Bible.

> 35 On that day, when evening came, He [Jesus] said to them, "Let us go over to the other side."
>
> 36 Leaving the crowd, they took Him along with them in the boat, just as He was; and other boats were with Him.
>
> 37 And there arose a fierce gale of wind, and the waves

were breaking over the boat so much that the boat was already filling up.

38 Jesus Himself was in the stern, asleep on the cushion; and they woke Him and said to Him, "Teacher, do You not care that we are perishing?"

39 And He got up and rebuked the wind and said to the sea, "Hush, be still." And the wind died down and it became perfectly calm.

40 And He said to them, "Why are you afraid? Do you still have no faith?"

41 They became very much afraid and said to one another, "Who then is this, that even the wind and the sea obey Him?"

Let's observe this text by asking some of the investigative type questions we've already talked about—the five Ws and H (who, what, when, where, why, and how).

Who is in the boat?

Where are they going?

What happens to the boat?

Why do the disciples wake Jesus? And what do they say to Him?

In verses 39-40, how does Jesus respond to the situation? To the wind and waves? To the disciples?

See how easy that is! You simply read the text looking for key words and then ask the five Ws and H questions, and there you have it. Now that we've observed the text, let's interpret it and apply it to our lives.

One of the most important things to discover when attempting to interpret a text is *context*. As I said before, context is simply the verses surrounding the passage you are studying. In this case it would be Mark chapters 3 through 5.

FAMILY FEUD

In chapter 3 we see Jesus healing people and driving out demons. In verse 11 we see the demons proclaiming that Jesus is the Son of God. We also see Jesus building His team of disciples and redefining His family. At the end of chapter 3, in verse 35, Jesus says, "Whoever does the will of God, he is my brother and sister and mother." It sounds like His family is growing. You would think that a man who brings healing and transformation to the people would be welcomed with open arms, wouldn't you? Not necessarily!

Jesus is upsetting some of the religious—let's say falsely religious—people. Mark 3:6 says, "The Pharisees went out and immediately began conspiring with the Herodians against Him, as to how they might destroy Him." And later in the chapter, these folk actually say that Jesus is working for the devil!

Skip over to chapter 5 and you discover that Jesus is continuing to heal and deliver people from demons.

So what is the context so far? Jesus is exercising His power and demonstrating that He is the Son of God. Now let's look at the context in chapter 4. One of the practices we teach here at Precept is to write notes in the margins of your Bible about what is happening in each paragraph or section. If you have a Bible with wide margins, it's easy to see the contents of a chapter by simply looking at your notes in the margin.

Looking at Mark 4, we discover that the majority of the chapter is not about Jesus doing miracles—healing or casting out demons. Instead, we find Jesus teaching. Jesus is teaching about the kingdom of God by using illustrations such as a sower casting seed in different types of soil, a lamp under a basket, a super-fast growing seed, and a tiny mustard seed that has tons of power. The last teaching before our text about faith is Jesus' parable about the mustard seed.

The mustard seed is the tiniest of seeds. Not much to look at. But plant it and watch out! It grows into a huge tree.

ANOTHER LESSON ON FAITH IN A BOAT

Then comes our story about the boat, the horrific storm, the supernatural act of Jesus, and the lack of faith in the disciples.

So let's interpret the story.

Jesus was on the road—teaching about God's kingdom and demonstrating His healing power. His power wasn't just a fluke of good fortune—a possible coincidence or a matter of good timing. He demonstrated His supernatural power to many different people in different situations. His teaching was so attractive that the crowds literally forced Him into a boat so that He could teach without being overrun by the surging multitudes.

After one such teaching session, He and His disciples set sail across the Sea of Galilee. When a major storm slammed into the little boat, the prospects for surviving didn't look too good. Would this be the end of the story? Would the headlines in the *Capernaum*

Times read: "Powerful Healer and Teacher Lost at Sea"? Would the Son of God perish in a storm?

Of course not. Nobody could ever take the life of Jesus from Him...unless and until He laid it down. But the disciples had forgotten who Jesus was.

GREATEST ENEMY OF FAITH IS FEAR

The circumstances that surrounded the disciples overrode their understanding of who was in the boat with them. They allowed what was seen to determine what couldn't be seen. They woke up their Master, who had been peacefully sleeping in the stern, but only after attempting to save themselves by madly bailing water. When they realized it was no use and that they were going to die, then finally they woke Jesus. Look again at verse 38. They said to Him, "Teacher, do You not care that we are perishing?"

"Don't You care? Are You for real? Come on! Are You God or not? Are You going to let us drown?"

Jesus stood up and simply said "Hush" to the winds and waves.

And immediately, that's exactly what happened. Everything went dead still.

What would you expect Jesus to say to His men after an incident like that? Maybe something like, "Thanks, guys. That was a close one!" In other words, wouldn't you have thought He had been "asleep at the wheel" and that the disciples actually saved Jesus, rather than the other way around?

But what He actually said to them was "Why are you afraid? *Do you still have no faith?*"

That question hit home. It was the nail in the coffin. The text tells us it was calm, quiet, and perfectly still out there on that lake. The disciples seemed to have been in shock. Verse 41 tells us that they became very afraid when they realized that even the wind and the sea obeyed Jesus.

But the question hung in the air—"Do you still have no faith?" What was Jesus asking of the disciples? What did He want them to know, to do? It looks as though Jesus wanted them not to panic—not to be afraid of death—but to realize that He was the Son of God and that He had complete control of everything. It was *wrong* to panic with Jesus in the boat!

Having faith would involve taking everything they knew about Jesus and then acting on it. Faith is the assurance that with Jesus, the very Son of God, in the boat, all was going according to His sovereign plan.

What would faith have looked like in this boat? "Faith is a refusal to panic...Faith is unbelief kept quiet, kept down."[12]

Let's explore this idea of having faith a bit further.

WHAT IS FAITH?

Read Hebrews 11:1, mark *faith,* and then list out what you learn.

> Now faith is the assurance of things hoped for, the
>
> conviction of things not seen.

Faith is:

Now read verse 6, and add to your list above what you learn about faith. Be sure to include in your list what one must believe about God. *Believe* is the verb form of the noun *faith* in the Greek language.

> And without faith it is impossible to please Him, for
>
> he who comes to God must believe that He is and that
>
> He is a rewarder of those who seek Him.

Let's look at some more of this chapter in the book of Hebrews to see what we can learn about faith. This chapter is often called the "Hall of Faith." In chapter 11 we read of the Old Testament heroes of the faith. As you read the passage below, you will see the phrase *by faith* several times. Mark this phrase as you marked *faith* earlier. Also, circle the name of the person being described and underline what you learn that the person did "by faith."

Hebrews 11:7-19

> 7 By faith Noah, being warned by God about things not yet seen, in reverence prepared an ark for the salvation of his household, by which he condemned the world, and became an heir of the righteousness which is according to faith.
>
> 8 By faith Abraham, when he was called, obeyed by going out to a place which he was to receive for an inheritance; and he went out, not knowing where he was going.
>
> 9 By faith he lived as an alien in the land of promise, as in a foreign land, dwelling in tents with Isaac and Jacob, fellow heirs of the same promise;
>
> 10 for he was looking for the city which has foundations, whose architect and builder is God.
>
> 11 By faith even Sarah herself received ability to conceive, even beyond the proper time of life, since she considered Him faithful who had promised.
>
> 12 Therefore there was born even of one man, and him as good as dead at that, as many descendants as the stars of heaven in number, and innumerable as the sand which is by the seashore.

13 All these died in faith, without receiving the promises, but having seen them and having welcomed them from a distance, and having confessed that they were strangers and exiles on the earth.

14 For those who say such things make it clear that they are seeking a country of their own.

15 And indeed if they had been thinking of that country from which they went out, they would have had opportunity to return.

16 But as it is, they desire a better country, that is, a heavenly one. Therefore God is not ashamed to be called their God; for He has prepared a city for them.

17 By faith Abraham, when he was tested, offered up Isaac, and he who had received the promises was offering up his only begotten son;

18 it was he to whom it was said, "In Isaac your descendants shall be called."

19 He considered that God is able to raise people even from the dead, from which he also received him back as a type.

What did you learn about Noah's faith?

What different actions and beliefs did you see Abraham and Sarah exercise "by faith"?

Now let's look at what we learn about Moses and what he did "by faith." Continue to mark as you did earlier in Hebrews 11.

23 By faith Moses, when he was born, was hidden for three months by his parents, because they saw he was a beautiful child; and they were not afraid of the king's edict.

24 By faith Moses, when he had grown up, refused to be called the son of Pharaoh's daughter,

25 choosing rather to endure ill-treatment with the people of God than to enjoy the passing pleasures of sin,

26 considering the reproach of Christ greater riches than the treasures of Egypt; for he was looking to the reward.

27 By faith he left Egypt, not fearing the wrath of the king; for he endured, as seeing Him who is unseen.

28 By faith he kept the Passover and the sprinkling of the blood, so that he who destroyed the firstborn would not touch them.

29 By faith they passed through the Red Sea as though

they were passing through dry land; and the Egyptians, when they attempted it, were drowned.

List what you learned about Moses and what he was able to do and believe "by faith."

FAITH THAT INSPIRES

Just reading these stories has a way of charging my battery! To read about men and women who have taken God's Word seriously and stepped forward to confront life's challenges with courage and boldness inspires me to follow in their footsteps. Does it have that effect on you? You may want to take some time and read the Old Testament stories referred to in Hebrews 11. If your Bible has cross-references in the margin, that's an easy way to track down these exciting true-life accounts.

Okay, let's review. *Faith*—it means to trust in God. It means to have assurance of God's Word, His promises, even when our circumstances seem to be screaming the very opposite. Remember what you read in Hebrews 11:1: Faith is the assurance of things hoped for (which means they were promised to you) and the conviction of things not seen (which means the answer or solution to your dilemma may not be apparent at the time).

You learned in Hebrews 11:6 that it's impossible to please God without faith. This means that faith isn't just for mature or super-Christians; it is for every believer in Jesus Christ. We also learned that to have faith we must believe that God is for real, that the God of the Bible is alive and active in your life. And we are told in verse 6 that we must believe that God will reward us if we seek Him. Seeking God, then, as demonstrated by the people in Hebrews 11, means that we are to exercise our faith—to live *by* faith. To walk according to His Word, to think and act according to the truth.

Finally for today, let's look at how we gain access to this faith. Ephesians 2:8-9 says:

> 8 For by grace you have been saved through faith; and
>
> that not of yourselves, it is the gift of God;
>
> 9 not as a result of works, so that no one may boast.

Using the words above, how does a person come to salvation?

So how do you get faith? Do you discover it? Can you earn it somehow? Do you inherit it from your parents? No. It's a gift. God gives it to you. You don't get saved by your works, by trying hard enough to be accepted by God. You can't clean up your act well enough and long enough to earn your salvation. This passage teaches us that it is not achieved in that way. Why? So that you will never be able to boast about your salvation, as though it were something you achieved on your own. In fact, no one could have achieved it but God alone.

Often when I hear this passage taught, the teacher stops with verse 9 and ignores the following verse. Ephesians 2:10, however, tells us *why* we are saved. Here's the reason:

> For we are His workmanship, created in Christ Jesus
> for good works, which God prepared beforehand so
> that we would walk in them.

We are saved to do what God has created us to do—walk by faith in the good works He has laid out for us. Before we even made our appearance in this world, God already had a plan for us, a plan to walk in obedience to Him. This doesn't mean just a general obedience but rather obedience in specific works that God has "prepared beforehand" for us.

CRAFTED BY GOD

He tells us that we are His workmanship. I love that term. His workmanship means that He—as our Creator and Redeemer, our Lord and Savior—has uniquely crafted us to be engaged in the good He has ready and waiting for us!

The Scriptures clearly teach that we must have faith. There's no way around it, and there are no other options. Without faith it is impossible to please Him (Hebrews 11:6). Why? Because without faith we're walking according to our wisdom instead of His, and it's no match!

But knowing about something and actually doing it can be miles and miles apart, can't it? As you work on growing strong spiritually, this is one area where I can guarantee that God will stretch you.

As I write these words, the leadership here at Precept Ministries is working through some tough financial times in our ministry. Donations are dropping quickly, as the financial outlook in our whole nation looks uncertain—with no relief on the horizon.

So what should we do?

I'll tell you exactly what we *will* do. We will continue to look to our Lord Jesus in faith and great expectation for what He will accomplish on our behalf. This is an adventure, and there's no room for panic. The days ahead are going to be exciting.

Jesus is in the boat with us!

TAKE AWAY

Do you understand faith? Faith isn't just hoping. Faith is trusting, believing, and acting upon the solid truth that Jesus is God and He is with you.

Why be afraid? Jesus is in the boat with you!

What Is So Great About Being a Slave?

Davɪᴅ

Today is the last day! Or is it?

We hope you won't let the great progress of the past 27 days grow cold. Our desire is that you will use this time we've spent together as a springboard for your spiritual growth. Take what you have learned and grow with it. If you want to seal these truths in your heart and mind and life, we suggest you start a small group and study this together. Go deeper with others. Disciple. Share it. Teach it to others.

So Who Are You?

We started off this journey making introductions—to God. We were introduced to God the Father, God the Son, and God the Holy Spirit. Today, we finish by introducing you to yourself.

"What does that mean? I know me. I know who I am. So why the need for an introduction?"

I want you to see who *you* are in light of all that you have studied these past four weeks. Ready for it?

You are a slave.

Let me explain. When the Bible was written, slaves were common. A slave was one who was purchased by another, captured in war, or was indebted to the master. The slave of biblical times was completely sold out to his master. A slave wasn't an employee who worked for a wage and had his or her own life; rather, a slave was a possession of the master. All rights were relinquished to the master and all ownership of possessions was turned over. The slave had nothing of his own. The daily agenda was set by the master.

"Wait, I don't want to be a slave! I want to make my own decisions, have my own stuff. I want to take care of myself!"

Really?

Do you really trust yourself to set the right agenda? Do you know what the future holds? Do you honestly think you can decide what is best for you—for today and for the years to come?

Do you have it all figured out? Are you immune to family crises, stock market crashes, war, disease, and other catastrophic events?

A GOOD SLAVE MUST HAVE A GOOD MASTER

So whom can you trust? Whom can you rely on to provide, protect, and be with you every step of the way? Your Master—the Almighty God of heaven and earth, the King of kings and Lord of lords, the Creator of all that exists, the Sustainer of all life on earth, who holds your molecules together, giving you each and every breath of air you take. This is who you can trust.

Let's look at some Scripture on being a slave.

Deuteronomy was written to the people of Israel as they journeyed from Egypt to the Promised Land. In this book God gives them rules to live by and shows them the way life is to be as the people of God. He sets their values and agenda before them in clear language.

Read Deuteronomy 15:12-17 and color the references to *slave* and synonymous phrases such as *sold to, servant, maidservant;* also include the pronouns *he* and *him.*

12 "If your kinsman, a Hebrew man or woman, is sold to

you, then he shall serve you six years, but in the sev-

enth year you shall set him free.

13 "When you set him free, you shall not send him away

empty-handed.

14 "You shall furnish him liberally from your flock

and from your threshing floor and from your wine vat; you shall give to him as the LORD your God has blessed you.

15 "You shall remember that you were a slave in the land of Egypt, and the LORD your God redeemed you; therefore I command you this today.

16 "It shall come about if he says to you, 'I will not go out from you,' because he loves you and your household, since he fares well with you;

17 then you shall take an awl and pierce it through his ear into the door, and he shall be your servant forever. Also you shall do likewise to your maidservant."

How was the slave to be treated?

What was the master to do for the slave when giving him his freedom? Does this sound different from modern slavery, such as the slaves who were brought to America from Africa experienced?

What was the slave's option at the time of release?

How long was the slave committing himself to the master (verse 17)? How was this type of slave identified? (See verse 17 for the action taken to mark the slave.)

True Confession

I recall wanting an earring as a teenager. Not two earrings like a girl, just one. I can't remember which ear. I was on a summer missions trip to the Bahamas, of all places, when I finally got my earring.

"Bahamas? Are you serious? That was a missions trip? Are you sure it wasn't a vacation?"

Yes, it was missions. We spent our time in the schools doing evangelism with the students. The schools allowed us to come in because the teachers were finished with their curriculum but the students were required by law to stay in school one more month.

I had a friend pierce my ear. I made the mistake of telling my dad about it on the phone. The very next day I received a telegram. (This was before the days of e-mail and cell phones.) The telegram simply read, "TAKE OUT THE EARRING." The command was followed by several Bible references that spoke about defiling the body.

Now you have to remember that I was raised on the campus of Precept Ministries. I knew how to study the Bible. I was familiar with the texts. So I was tempted to break out my concordance and do my own word study on *earrings*. Of course, this text in Deuteronomy would have been my place to start. I can just hear it now. "Dad, I'm a bondservant to God. Forever. My earring proves it." But I came to my senses, realizing I would only be trying to justify my desires and not the wishes of my father. Plus—if Dad said it, I'd better obey. And so that day, I took out my earring and let the hole heal closed.

But in the book of Deuteronomy we learn that the slave for life marked himself in this way to show that his master was good. If in the market you saw a slave with a big hole in his ear, you knew he wasn't making a fashion statement. He was the property for life of a good master.

ONCE A SLAVE, ALWAYS A SLAVE—THANKFULLY

I heard John MacArthur preach on this subject once. He pointed out that in the Greek New Testament the word for "servant" and "bondservant" were one and the same—*doulos* (pronounced doo-loss). A *doulos* was one who belonged to the master. According to MacArthur, *doulos* was never translated as anything besides "slave." Yet in 1560, when the Geneva Bible was being translated, *doulos* was translated as "servant."

There seems to be a big difference between *servant* and *slave*. A servant is more like an employee who has some rights of his own and can seek employment with another person at his own will. But a slave has no such rights. A slave belongs to the master.

YOU ARE IN GOOD COMPANY

You might think that the leaders of the early church would hold claim to their position of authority when addressing the church in the epistles of the New Testament. Instead Paul, James, Peter, Jude, and John introduce themselves as a *doulos* of the Lord Jesus Christ:

- *Romans 1:1*—"Paul, a **bond-servant** [*doulos*] of Christ Jesus, called as an apostle, set apart for the gospel of God."

- *Philippians 1:1*—"Paul and Timothy, **bond-servants** [*doulos*] of Christ Jesus, to all the saints in Christ Jesus who are in Philippi, including the overseers and deacons."

- *Galatians 1:10*—"For am I now seeking the favor of men, or of God? Or am I striving to please men? If I were still trying to please men, I would not be a **bond-servant** [*doulos*] of Christ."

- *Titus 1:1*—"Paul, a **bond-servant** [*doulos*] of God and an apostle of Jesus Christ, for the faith of those chosen of God and the knowledge of the truth which is according to godliness.

- *James 1:1*—"James, a **bond-servant** [*doulos*] of God and of the Lord Jesus Christ, to the twelve tribes who are dispersed abroad: Greetings."

- *2 Peter 1:1*—"Simon Peter, a **bond-servant** [*doulos*] and apostle of Jesus Christ, to those who have received a faith of the same kind as ours, by the righteousness of our God and Savior, Jesus Christ."

- *Jude 1*—"Jude, a **bond-servant** [*doulos*] of Jesus Christ, and brother of James, to those who are the called, beloved in God the Father, and kept for Jesus Christ."

- *Revelation 1:1*—"The Revelation of Jesus Christ, which God gave Him to show to His **bond-servants** [*doulos*], the things which must soon take place; and He sent and communicated it by His angel to His **bond-servant** [*doulos*] John."

THE GREATEST SLAVE

But the greatest of these bond-servants is Jesus Himself. Read Philippians 2:5-8:

5 Have this attitude in yourselves which was also in Christ Jesus,

6 who, although He existed in the form of God, did not regard equality with God a thing to be grasped,

7 but emptied Himself, taking the form of a **bond-servant** [*doulos*], and being made in the likeness of men.

8 Being found in appearance as a man, He humbled Himself by becoming obedient to the point of death, even death on a cross.

Wow! Jesus—the second person of the Trinity, God the Son, the Creator and Redeemer, the King above all kings, the Mighty Conqueror of Revelation 19—took on the form of a *doulos*! That explains the conversation Jesus had in the Garden of Gethsemane just before He went to the cross to die.

Matthew 26:36-39

36 Then Jesus came with them to a place called Gethsemane, and said to His disciples, "Sit here while I go over there and pray."

37 And He took with Him Peter and the two sons of Zebedee, and began to be grieved and distressed.

38 Then He said to them, "My soul is deeply grieved, to the point of death; remain here and keep watch with Me."

39 And He went a little beyond them, and fell on His face and prayed, saying, "My Father, if it is possible, let this cup pass from Me; yet not as I will, but as You will."

Jesus said to His Father, "Not as I will, but as You will." He took on the form of a servant—a slave, a *doulos*—that you and I might be saved. Take a minute to thank God for this incredible sacrifice on your behalf.

So you are a slave.

Considering who your Master is, that's not so bad, is it?

Paul teaches in Romans 10:9, "If you confess with your mouth Jesus as Lord, and believe in your heart that God raised Him from the dead, you will be saved." The Greek term translated "Lord" is *kyrios* (pronounced cur-ree-oss). *Kyrios* means "supreme ruler over all." To understand Jesus as *kyrios* we must understand ourselves as *doulos*. Do you see the relationship? We are slaves and Jesus is supreme Lord. To be a slave of the supreme Lord, ruler over all, is to be in the best position you could wish for. Your Master is powerful. Your Master is good.

Romans is my favorite book of the New Testament, perhaps of the entire Bible. I'm not sure if it's because it was the book I was studying when God called me into full-time ministry, showing me my spiritual gift of teaching, or if it's because the content just blows me away. Either way, I love Romans.

TRUTH TAUGHT EVEN IN THE STRUCTURE OF THE BOOK

The book of Romans has 16 chapters. The first 11 chapters are packed with statements of truth, which we call doctrine. There are very few instructions, commands, or warnings in the first 11 chapters. But starting in chapter 12, the instructions come flooding into the text. The last four chapters brim with instructions, commands, and warnings. It's as if Paul is teaching the reader that truth comes first and obedience second. The structure of 11 chapters versus 4 chapters shows that truth and doctrine matter greatly in the Christian's life. The structure of Romans also teaches that we must know the truth before we can live it out.

So many Christians burn out quickly in their journey because they try to be good without understanding God's Word. They simply think they can read a Bible verse a day and survive. But that's not true, my friend. The Bible talks about meditating on God's Word, which means to soak in it, study it, memorize it, and process it regularly.

Let's look at the transition Paul makes from the truth of Romans 1–11 and the application of truth in chapters 12–16:

Romans 11:33–12:2

> 33 Oh, the depth of the riches both of the wisdom and knowledge of God! How unsearchable are His judgments and unfathomable His ways!
>
> 34 For who has known the mind of the Lord, or who became His counselor?
>
> 35 Or who has first given to Him that it might be paid back to him again?
>
> 36 For from Him and through Him and to Him are all things. To Him be the glory forever. Amen.
>
> 12:1 Therefore I urge you, brethren, by the mercies of God, to present your bodies a living and holy sacrifice, acceptable to God, which is your spiritual service of worship.
>
> 2 And do not be conformed to this world, but be transformed by the renewing of your mind, so that you may prove what the will of God is, that which is good and acceptable and perfect.

Let's start by observing Romans 11:33-36. What do you learn about the truth of God—the wisdom and knowledge of God?

What is Paul's response to the truth in verse 36?

WHAT IS THE *THEREFORE* THERE FOR?

Now let's look at our response to the truth Paul calls for in Romans 12:1-2. I call it a response because Paul begins this section with the word "therefore." If you've ever been involved with Kay Arthur and Precept Ministries, then you will know that whenever you see the word "therefore" in Scripture, you need to ask what it's "there for." "Therefore" is a term of conclusion. "Therefore" marks the transition from the lesson to the application, the truth to the trust.

First, I want you to see what Paul means when he says "by the mercies of God." Paul is saying in this phrase, "Now, *because of* or *through* the mercies of God"—what he has been writing about in the first 11 chapters of Romans—present yourselves to God. We are to present ourselves to God because of His grace.

Second, I want you to see that Paul is "urging" you to present yourselves to God. He is not suggesting but urging. Do you feel the importance of this call to application? Paul is saying, "God's wisdom and knowledge are amazing (as he declares in Romans 11:33-36), so let's do something in response. Let me urge you—strongly urge you—to respond by presenting yourselves to God."

But how are we to present ourselves to God? Partially present? Does this mean God gets my Sundays only? Am I joining some kind of association called Christianity that requires ten percent of my finances as dues and at least one day a week for worship?

No! Look at verse 1 again—"to present your bodies"—how?—"as a living and holy *sacrifice*." Sacrifice? What does that mean?

In the Old Testament, God called for His people Israel to offer sacrifices. The item to be sacrificed was usually something of great value, such as an animal that was given to God on the altar. By "given" I mean it was killed and placed on the altar.

The sacrifice has no rights; it can't make any demands on its master. The sacrifice gives all of itself on the altar. Verse 2 tells us the process of presenting ourselves as a sacrifice to God:

> And do not be conformed to this world, but be trans-
> formed by the renewing of your mind, so that you
> may prove what the will of God is, that which is good
> and acceptable and perfect.

CONFORMED AND TRANSFORMED

"Conformed" implies being shaped by outside forces, like clay being squeezed in the hands of a potter. Paul is saying, "Don't let the world with its values shape you like itself."

"Transformed" comes from the word "metamorphosis." "Meta-morphosis" is the process that changes a stubby, grubby caterpillar into a beautiful, free-flying butterfly. Paul is telling us to let the truths of God renew our minds and change our hearts and beliefs—transforming us from the inside out.

THIS IS SPIRITUAL GROWTH

To grow spiritually strong starts with knowing who God is, studying what He teaches in His Word about how we are to live, talking to Him in prayer, confessing our sins, and understanding who we are in Christ.

We are slaves, yes, but slaves of an incredible Master, the Lord God Almighty.

Now, my fellow slave, present yourself wholly and completely to God as a living sacrifice. Dig deep into His Word and let it shape you from within, that you may know life that is truly life.

A TESTIMONY FROM KAY

An exam was facing me the next morning; studying was not a choice. After tucking Mark and Tom in bed, I spread my books on the kitchen table in our small home. Little did I realize that this night would provide an anchor that would hold me in the fierce winds of temptation. It would be a night I would never forget.

Settled at the table, I picked up the textbook I was to be tested on: *Life on the Highest Plane* by Ruth Paxson. I don't remember anything about the book except Romans 12:1-2. In those verses the apostle Paul was begging me—pleading with me—to present my body to my God as a living sacrifice.

And for whatever reason, on that particular night Paul's words pierced my heart.

> Therefore I urge you, brethren, by the mercies of God,
> to present your bodies a living and holy sacrifice,
> acceptable to God, which is your spiritual service of
> worship. And do not be conformed to this world, but
> be transformed by the renewing of your mind, so that
> you may prove what the will of God is, that which is
> good and acceptable and perfect (Romans 12:1-2).

From what I read, I understood that it was "once and for all"— that once my all was put on the altar, it was done, never to be changed, never to be rescinded, never to be redone or rededicated. What touched the altar was holy. It belonged to God.

I was a living sacrifice, a holy sacrifice, offering to God the life He had redeemed with the blood of His Son. It was to be His, not mine. What He was asking was reasonable, so very logical in the light of so great a salvation. If I really loved God, if I really respected Him and honored Him as God, then I would worship Him—show His worth, His worthiness—in such an act.

I don't know the day or month, but I know that on that very evening I consciously put myself on His altar, and in His grace, He has kept me there.

Oh, Beloved, the way to strength is the way of sacrifice—your body, your life presented to Him, at one point in time, once and for all. It is your reasonable service, your act of worship, your voluntary offering. Without it, I don't believe you'll ever be all you could be for Him.

> For from Him and through Him and to Him are all things. To Him be the glory forever. Amen (Romans 11:36).

So Where Do You Go from Here?

We recommend that you continue this journey with another 28-day book. Start with *Lord, Teach Me to Study the Bible in 28 Days*. In this book, you will learn how to study the Bible in a way that will change your life. We honestly believe that. We have seen this transformation happen thousands of times with people in many different contexts, countries, and stages of life.

When you finish that book, take the next leg of the journey and read *Lord, Teach Me to Pray in 28 Days*. This book will help you to learn how to talk to God and listen to Him in prayer.

We are so excited you have come this far. May God now bless you and keep you; may He make His face to shine upon you both now and forever more. Amen.

"Finally, be strong in the Lord and in the strength of His might" (Ephesians 6:10).

1. Kay Arthur and Pete DeLacy, *Key Principles of Biblical Fasting*. To obtain a copy for yourself, visit our website: www.Precept.org.

2. Precept Upon Precept courses are in-depth studies of different books of the Bible. These studies will take you further in your understanding because you will use the inductive method of study. To learn how to get started in a study, visit our website: www.Precept.org.

3. I've written a study called *Lord, I Need Grace to Make It Today,* and it has helped so many. Teaching CDs and DVDs are available. A Gold Medallion winner.

4. In 1991, I wrote *Lord, Is It Warfare? Teach Me to Stand*. It's one of the most popular studies led by our Precept students and teachers in prisons.

5. Spiros Zodhiates, *The Complete Word Study Dictionary: New Testament,* electronic ed. (Chattanooga, TN: AMG Publishers, 2000, 1992, 1993).

6. Alvin J. Schmidt, *Under the Influence: How Christianity Transformed Civilization* (Grand Rapids, MI: Zondervan, 2001), 80.

7. Ibid.

8. Edward Gibbon, *The History of the Decline and Fall of the Roman Empire* (reprint, London: Penguin Books, 1994), 813.

9. Schmidt, *Under the Influence*, 83.

10. You can order *The Truth About Sex* online at www.precept.org or call 1-800-763-8280. The publisher is WaterBrook Press.

11. These can all be ordered by calling 1-800-763-8280 or going online: www.precept.org. Ordering from us helps our ministry reach others. These studies are available in numerous languages. We're in 150 countries and 70 languages, and your participation in Precept Ministries International helps us continue and expand this needed ministry of establishing people in God's Word, teaching and helping them to discover truth for themselves and to go deeper and disciple others.

12. D. Martyn Lloyd-Jones, *Spiritual Depression: Its Causes and Cure* (Grand Rapids, MI: Wm. B. Eerdmans Publishing Co., 1965), 143.

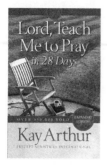

Lord, Teach Me to Pray in 28 Days
Kay Arthur

This bestselling 28-day study (more than 525,000 copies sold in English alone!) will give you practical insights to help you know how to pray, what to pray, and what to expect when you pray.

This look at biblical prayer is refreshingly simple and exceedingly powerful—and it can transform the way you live and pray. Ideal for individual or group study, and a classic resource for any home or church library.

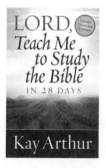

Lord, Teach Me to Study the Bible in 28 Days
Kay Arthur

Kay leads you into the fascinating world of inductive Bible study, where God Himself becomes the teacher (Psalm 119:102). This book teaches you how to study Scripture and specifically mark the text to unlock its meaning. In just 28 days you'll learn how to

- study the Bible book by book and understand what you're reading

- recognize key words and concepts in the Bible

- discover the main point of any passage of Scripture

- discern God's purpose and apply life-changing truths to your everyday life

This is a very practical, hands-on, learn-by-doing book, perfect for individuals and small groups.

CHANGING THE WAY
PEOPLE STUDY GOD'S WORD

"Inductive study of the Bible is the best way to discover scriptural truth…There is no jewel more precious than that which you have mined yourself."

—HOWARD HENDRICKS

THIS GOLD MEDALLION WINNER IS UNIQUE AMONG STUDY BIBLES.

Every feature is designed to help you gain a more intimate understanding of God and His Word. This study Bible, the *only* one based entirely on the inductive study approach, shows you how to discover truth for yourself book by book.